The Life and Times of Gerald de Cruz

The **ISEAS–Yusof Ishak Institute** (formerly Institute of Southeast Asian Studies) was established as an autonomous organization in 1968. It is a regional centre dedicated to the study of socio-political, security and economic trends and developments in Southeast Asia and its wider geostrategic and economic environment. The Institute's research programmes are the Regional Economic Studies (RES, including ASEAN and APEC), Regional Strategic and Political Studies (RSPS), and Regional Social and Cultural Studies (RSCS).

ISEAS Publishing, an established academic press, has issued more than 2,000 books and journals. It is the largest scholarly publisher of research about Southeast Asia from within the region. ISEAS Publishing works with many other academic and trade publishers and distributors to disseminate important research and analyses from and about Southeast Asia to the rest of the world.

The Life and Times of Gerald de Cruz

ASAD-UL IQBAL LATIF

First published in Singapore in 2015 by ISEAS Publishing
ISEAS–Yusof Ishak Institute
30 Heng Mui Keng Terrace
Singapore 119614

E-mail: publish@iseas.edu.sg
Website: <http://bookshop.iseas.edu.sg>

ISEAS Library Cataloguing-in-Publication Data

The Life and Times of Gerald de Cruz : a Singaporean of Many Worlds / edited by Asad-ul Iqbal Latif.

1. De Cruz, Gerald, 1920–1991.
2. Eurasians—Singapore—Biography.
3. Politicians—Singapore—Biography.
4. Nationalists—Singapore—Biography.
5. Communists—Singapore—Biography.
6. Journalists—Singapore—Biography.

I. Latif, Asad-ul Iqbal.

DS610.63 D29L72 2015

ISBN 978-981-4620-68-0 (soft cover)
ISBN 978-981-4620-69-7 (e-book, PDF)

Typeset by Superskill Graphics Pte Ltd
Printed in Singapore by Mainland Press Pte Ltd

For

Gayathri, Roshini, Vandana, Pavithra and Varad Kailash

members of a generation of
Singaporeans who are beneficiaries of
the legacy of Gerald de Cruz's life's work
and his vision of a multiracial Singapore

CONTENTS

PREFACE

Gerald de Cruz was an *interstitial* figure in Singapore's history after World War II. As a Eurasian, a nationalist, a communist and then a democratic socialist, as a journalist and a writer, he represents the overlapping energies of these spheres which the politics of the time brought together, often in opposition and conflict. He never rose to high political office, but his commitment to progressive ideas and movements speaks of a man of integrity trying to stay true to the roles that he had chosen for himself. This book seeks to portray his place in time for a younger generation of Singaporeans who might not be aware of how political choices were made at an important juncture of Singapore's history.

This book is based primarily on material drawn from Gerald de Cruz, Oral History Interview, by Foo Kim Leng; the Gerald de Cruz Papers deposited at the Institute of Southeast Asian Studies, Singapore; and his book, *Colliding Worlds: Memoirs of a Singapore Maverick*, a re-issue of *Rojak Rebel: Memoirs of a Singapore Maverick* with four new essays. His books on Malayan independence, nationalism and communism — the latter two based on his numerous talks delivered as a lecturer for the Political Study Centre — have also been consulted extensively.

I would like to record my gratitude to the former Director of the Institute of Southeast Asian Studies, Ambassador K. Kesavapany, who entrusted the writing of the book to me; and the present Director, Ambassador Tan Chin Tiong, under whom I completed it.

I would like to thank Mr Pitt Kuan Wah, Head of the ISEAS Library, and Ms D. Gandhimathy, Senior Manager at the library, for their invaluable assistance with research; Mr Ng Kok Kiong, Head of ISEAS Publishing, for his encouragement; Mr Stephen Logan, Editor – Special Projects, for his close attention to details of fact and nuances of style. This is a much better book than it was as a manuscript because of him.

Gerald de Cruz's family, particularly his daughter, Justice Judith Prakash; his son-in-law, Mr Jaya Prakash; and his son, Ambassador Simon de Cruz, provided invaluable help in fleshing out many aspects of his life. I thank Joshua de Cruz, a doctoral student at the University of London, for sourcing material on Gerald de Cruz's political activities from British archives.

FAMILY TREE

Gerald Evelyn de Cruz

20 February 1920 – 9 December 1991

Parents

Cecil Thomas de Cruz and Evelyn Woodford

Siblings

Dudley Aloysius, Guy Anthony, Hazel

Wives

Coral Alma Phipps, Maimunah Mohammad

Children

Judith Evelyn (m. Jaya Prakash)
Simon Tensing (m. Kwah Poh Choo)
Adam

Grandchildren

Gayathri Prakash Nair, Roshini Prakash Nair
Vandana Prakash Nair, Pavithra Prakash Nair

Great-grandchild

Varad Kailash Karthikeyan

Chapter 1

DON DE CRUZ DE LA SINGAPURA

Gerald de Cruz wrote to his daughter, Judith, on 17 November 1975, saying that he envied her watching again the film, "Man of La Mancha". Don Quixote's face is "as pasty as used canvas shoes; his walk almost as faltering as a drunk's; his spear always getting in the way of gates or bags of flour; and his sword, if it can be called that, looking like the first cousin to prehistoric man's first attempt at a corkscrew". Unlike Superman, who represents escape from the times and from reality, the "feeble, often ridiculous and frequently derided" figure of Don Quixote enchants people because they can recognize something of themselves in him. Born into what his creator, Miguel de Cervantes, calls a discourteous world, Don Quixote embodies the need for humans to meet the taunts of discourtesy. Prisoner of illusions himself, as every man is, the "sad and silly Knight" tilts at windmills. But why? Cervantes, wounded and captured in war and sold off into slavery before his family ransomed him at the cost of its financial ruin, experiences evil first-hand. However, he is interested in knowing, not why men die at the hands of evil, but why they have lived at all. They live, de Cruz avers, to confront the "distortions of reality which make it difficult to become human". By proclaiming what it was like to be human in the charged sixteenth century, Don Quixote the Castilian not only became the hero of a great literary creation, but also immortal. "It does not matter a tinker's damn that we are weak", de Cruz says of Don Quixote's sentimentality and delusions. "What matters is the direction in which our lives are pointed." That is the lasting legacy of Cervantes' canonical creation, *El ingenioso hidalgo don Quijote de la Mancha — The Ingenious Gentleman Don Quixote of La Mancha.*

The introspective intensity of de Cruz's engagement with Don Quixote suggests a degree of fellow feeling that could have come only from a shared experience of life preserved over four intervening centuries. Both were adventurous, astonishingly and sometimes dangerously so. De Cruz's amazing decision to take his wife-to-be, Coral, on a trip to the Kremlin to convince its amiable inhabitants to call off the armed uprising in Malaya does prove that truth can be stranger than fiction, especially since he hardly had money for the journey. His fortunes on that remarkable expedition, which naturally soon got derailed yet opened up new vistas for him and his steady but equally adventurous companion, would have made a worthy chapter in a modern rendition of *Don Quixote.* He probably was the only Eurasian communist from Singapore to have experienced a proper Catholic marriage in Karachi while the secret police were watching him, and he was almost run over by a capitalist's car as he crossed the road to buy the wedding ring. But in de Cruz's remarkable life, as in his knightly predecessor's, the improbable was a standing invitation to the possible. Reality was an inconvenience that both treated with genial nonchalance.

That nonchalance, however, was but a softer aspect of a life lived seriously, vividly and to the full. De Cruz contributed to society across a wide variety of fronts — community life, teaching, politics, the labour movement, voluntary service and journalism. *A Varied Life*.

De Cruz was fifty-five when he wrote to his daughter. Confronting reality had become second nature to him by then. Born into a Eurasian family in Singapore in 1920, he contested his ethnicity because of the privileges it derived from its affiliation with British colonial rule. Rejecting his father's ethnic faith in the British Empire, de Cruz sought a place in multiracial Singapore. He denied the agency of race because it obscured the fundamentally formative influence of society on an individual's self-awareness. As chairman of the Eurasian Progressive Movement in 1945, he placed his intellect and keen sense of history in the service of his community, which he sought to bring firmly within the mainstream of post-colonial history.

De Cruz practised what he believed in. When, during World War II, imperial Japan invaded and occupied Malaya and Singapore, he took the extraordinary step of joining the Japanese-supported Indian National Army (INA) to eject British colonialism from India. The Japanese, who had treated the Chinese with particular brutality because of their association with China, had targeted Eurasians because of their identification with the British. Yet, de Cruz made common cause with the INA because to him the political imperative of fighting colonialism took precedence over even the horrendous Japanese assault on his Eurasian identity. Those years were the beginning of a lifelong friendship with the INA military officer Inayatullah Hassan, who later settled in Pakistan and hosted the de Cruzes in Karachi. De Cruz's fascination for the people and the ways of the subcontinent led him to name his son Simon Tensing, after the Nepalese climber of Mount Everest.

De Cruz gravitated towards the Malayan Communist Party (MCP) and its allied organizations in their struggle against the returning British after the war. He was a founder member of the Malayan Democratic Union (MDU) in 1945, he became a cadre member of the MCP in February 1947, and played an influential role in politics as Executive Secretary of the Pan-Malayan Council of Joint Action in 1947–48. The product of a conservative Catholic upbringing, de Cruz had contemplated taking Holy Orders as a teenager. But he broke intellectually with the Church when a local priest rebuffed his religious doubts and questioning of ecclesiastical authority. His political doubts, particularly over the MCP's adoption of a strategy of armed revolt in Malaya in 1948, in turn led him to reject the party, which appeared to him to be a kind of secular church jealous of its monopoly of ideological truth and protective of its hierarchic authority. Repudiating church and party was of a piece with de Cruz's rejection of the authoritarian paternalism which his father had represented within the family, particularly over his mother, whom he adored. It was only towards the end of de Cruz Senior's life that son sought to reconcile with father.

However, the departures from Catholicism and communism were not exercises in escapism. They were decisions that he took following his intense experience of both, and they led to other kinds of engagement and commitment. Although gifted with a buoyant nature that sought sunshine and the company of like-minded bohemians, he was never a bourgeois philistine. In the case of religion, he arrived at Islam, becoming Haji Karim Abdullah in 1968. He was drawn to Sufism and developed a close friendship with the Sufi scholar Idries Shah and his sister, Amina. Politically, he found sanctuary in the broad left. Recalled from Britain — where he had campaigned for the Labour Party, of which he had been a member from 1952 to 1956 — by Singapore's first Chief Minister, David Marshall, de Cruz became the Organizing Secretary of the Labour Front between 1956 and 1958. He found his true home in democratic socialism. His work in the 1960s for the Political Study Centre, which the People's Action Party government had set up to socialize civil servants into the realities of self-governing Singapore, saw him lecture passionately on democratic politics and ideological trends in world affairs. He enjoyed talking to pre-university students, who responded with a barrage of questions so numerous that he wrote books based on his talks and his answers to their questions. It was fitting that de Cruz, who had received a teacher's diploma in London in 1952, risen to being Principal of Osborne House, a school for intellectually challenged children in England, from 1952 to 1956, and had lectured at the Workers' Educational Association there from 1952 to 1956, should return to teaching back home. He lectured at the National Youth Leadership Institute from 1964 to 1969, the Department of Extra-Mural Studies at the University of Singapore from 1968, the Police Academy from 1966 to 1970 and the National Police Cadet Corps from 1970, and was Supervisor of Studies at the Singapore Command and Staff College from 1969 to 1971.

In his personal life he took to blood donation with a regularity that brought him (unsolicited though they were) silver, gold and platinum medals. He was also a founder member and the first chairman of the Singapore Association for Retarded Children. In 1964, its school was the only one of its kind in Malaysia to give the children, aged from five to fourteen, free training in personal hygiene and social adjustment. He was also an adviser to the Juvenile Court Magistrate from 1961 to 1965, and a member of the Singapore Council of Social Service from 1965 to 1966. His Papers — which contain typewritten notes on the Singapore Children's Society, the Association for the Retarded, the Association for the Blind, the Singapore Association for the Deaf, the Singapore Handicaps' Friendship Club, and the scale of the social welfare challenge — bear testimony to the painstaking research that accompanied his voluntary work.

Singapore's ejection from Malaysia hurt de Cruz deeply, but his mind soon focused on the challenges of building a multiracial meritocracy in the free nation. He felt empowered by the way in which Singapore was cementing its independence by trying to create a new society through legislative radicalism and egalitarian daring. He was less confident of the international situation, but he believed that non-alignment was the city-state's safest bet in the global jungle. De Cruz was eager to prove that the ideas of socialism could be achieved within a democratic framework in Singapore. Although his defence of democratic socialism was directed primarily at those who derided it as a bourgeois parliamentary sell-out to capitalism, his rancorous break with Marxism did spill over occasionally into his vituperative denunciation of Leninism and Maoism. There was nothing personal in this battle, however; its polemical argumentativeness was just Don de Cruz's way of leaving his mark on the contested realities of those burning times — just as the combative Man of La Mancha had once done.

De Cruz went on to translate some of his political ideas into practical ways of increasing the contribution of labour to Singapore's industrialization. His paper, presented to the seminal 1969 Modernization Seminar organized by the National Trades Union Congress, provides insights into how labour can improve its bargaining power with capital through education. What Singapore's workers did not need was a self-destructive spiral of industrial strikes and street violence that would merely drive away investment and deepen unemployment and underemployment. De Cruz was undoubtedly a revisionist in pushing this line, but he had no quarrel with the term, "revisionist", which he understood as a way for socialists to remain ideologically relevant by staying responsive to specific national conditions and changing times. Hence his interest in labour issues, which spanned his years as Assistant Secretary of the Pan-Malayan Federation of Trade Unions in Kuala Lumpur from 1946 to 1948; his role as a founder member of the Singapore Industrial Labour Organization (SILO) in 1969; his chairmanship of the Information and Publicity Committee of the National Trades Union Congress from 1970; and his work as Education Officer in SILO and the Pioneer Industries Employees' Union (PIEU) from 1971. His editorial skills joined hands with his labour sympathies in his work for *Perjuangan*, the NTUC's monthly journal, and *Labour News*, the monthly journal of SILO and PIEU.

De Cruz was a consummate journalist. He worked for *The Straits Times*, *The Malayan Standard* and *The Democrat* in the 1940s, was Assistant Far East Correspondent for the London (Sunday) *Observer* in Singapore from 1958 to 1964, worked for *The New Nation* as Diplomatic Editor and columnist in the 1970s, and contributed to *The Sarawak Tribune* in the 1980s. He excelled as a columnist, using words with some of the existential edginess that had guided the spear of his illustrious Castilian predecessor. His left-liberal instincts and progressive views made him an ideal commentator on the times, particularly in the 1970s. A believer in a robust society who had little patience for the self-regarding antics of the sex-drugs-drenched counter-culture, he nevertheless contemplated life around him with a profound sense of empathy and compassion as he witnessed ordinary individuals trying to live in extraordinary times.

De Cruz's Singapore years — the subject of this book — ended effectively in 1975, when he left to become a training consultant for the Sarawak Foundation at the invitation of the state's Chief Minister (and later Governor), Haji Abdul Rahman bin Ya'kub. That work would take him a decade. He had remarried after the death of Coral de Cruz. His second wife, Rokiah (Maimunah) bte Mohd, gave him a son, Adam, in 1971. De Cruz suffered two strokes, in 1982 and 1983, but his mental faculties were unimpaired, and he remained with the Foundation until he retired in 1985.

Gerald de Cruz passed away in Kuala Lumpur in 1991, and was buried in Johor's Kampong Singapura.

In a world of Supermen, he had remained a quixotic man, answerable to no one but himself.

Chapter 2

CHILDHOOD AND YOUTH

Gerald Evelyn de Cruz was born in Singapore on 20 February 1920. He announced his arrival with a bang. To celebrate the advent of Chinese New Year, the family's neighbours were exploding thousands of red packets of firecrackers. It was a fitting start to a life that would be marked by one explosion after another — personal, national and global.

Gerald de Cruz was born to Cecil Thomas de Cruz and Evelyn Woodford, into a staunchly Roman Catholic family of Eurasian ancestry. He was the eldest of four children, followed by two brothers, Dudley and Guy, and a sister, Hazel. His ancestors had arrived in Singapore in 1824, just five years after Stamford Raffles had founded the city. "On my father's side, we were a mixture of Portuguese and Irish and Indian, and some people say, some Persian blood too, which perhaps gives me my Semitic nose. On my mother's side, we were a mixture of English and Dutch and Chinese", he recalled.[1]

De Cruz's family was a lower-middle-class one. The whole of the land from East Coast Road to the sea and between Chapel Road and Sea Avenue had belonged to his mother's grandfather, who had given a third of it to the Roman Catholic Church. It built the Church of the Holy Family in Katong on that land. Town Eurasians lived mostly in Queen Street, but outside town the community congregated in two main areas. One was in Katong, where there were the Catholic Eurasians, and the other was at Serangoon and Upper Serangoon, where there were the Anglican and Methodist Eurasians. The latter considered themselves a cut above the others because they were of British stock, whereas the Catholics were of Portuguese descent.

Eurasians were not only early residents of Singapore, Myrna Braga-Blake writes, but they also made it their home. Thus, by 1931, 77 per cent of Singapore's Eurasians had been born in Singapore — more than twice the proportion of the locally born among the Chinese, and five times that of the Indian community. "In the characteristically migrant population of the time, Eurasians stood out as a community with Singaporean roots."[2] In the first half of the nineteenth century, Eurasians felt very much at home in Singapore, where wealth race and colour "were of little importance in the informality that characterised social life". But in the second half of the century, social life altered in Singapore when the numbers of Europeans grew as a result of the advent of steam vessels and the opening of the Suez Canal. Also, faster mail and the introduction of the telegraph gave Europeans access to news and ideas from Europe. "Cliques emerged in Singapore's social life", Braga-Blake writes. "The Europeans became snobbish and exclusive, and class divisions crystallised." The Eurasian position became ambiguous. Although they were employed in the civil service in large numbers because of their education and trustworthiness, they "were held in contempt and excluded from the social circles of the European ruling class".[3] There was an "assertion of Eurasian identity" during and after World War I. The Eurasian Association was set up in 1919 at a time when there was "an escalation of anti-Asian sentiment among Europeans manifest in 'the colour bar' which excluded non-Europeans from senior positions in the civil service. Eurasians were among those who suffered from this prejudice."[4] However, there also was "an implicit recognition" of Eurasians as second to only Europeans in the socially dominant English-speaking community.[5]

Many Eurasians tried to make a virtue of the necessity of these ambiguities. Although Eurasians "worked in the engine room of the British Empire as clerks of imperial enterprise", they nevertheless were "sufficiently privileged to adopt British customs and attitudes with the apparent consent of their imperial masters", Joshua de Cruz notes.[6] Even the Singapore Recreation Club, a Eurasian institution set up in 1883 in the face of the European exclusiveness of the Singapore Cricket Club and the Tanglin Club, replicated European social mores in its racial exclusiveness and prohibition of the entry of women.[7] "Many Eurasians tried to pass off as white and deny their Asian heritage", the writer adds.[8] In its backing of British rule, Eurasians contested any disagreements "within rather than outside the colonial framework", and "if at all, Eurasians agitated for reform rather than revolution".[9] Of course, that largely was true of the other communities as well, but the difference is Eurasians would come to be seen later as a community that had sought "favours and preferential treatment as a buffer community between the white and coloured races".[10] Even after the Japanese Occupation had destroyed the myth of British invincibility, Eurasians did not adandon the British Empire "the way the British Empire had abandoned them".[11] Before the debacle, there was no doubt that Eurasians were "both victims and beneficiaries of colonialism", but that "as progeny of European expansion they were active participants in the imperial project", Joshua de Cruz declares.[12]

The complicated racial and political relationships that pervaded the times complicated Gerald de Cruz's relationship with his father. The senior de Cruz made the white man his model and pursued the idea of white supremacy in even small matters. For example, he would grow very angry when Gerald, as a child, would greet the family's servants, cooks and maids with a "Good morning". His father believed that that was the wrong way to talk to servants: They should never be treated as if they were friends or acquaintances. Being on familiar terms with the lower orders apparently subverted the hierarchic stability of the colonial universe. When he found his son eating with his fingers, he called it a dirty native habit. Indeed, even when taking his son to school in little red "mosquito-buses" that could carry up to nine passengers, he would not step in if more than half the occupants were natives. So Gerald often missed many buses and would be late for school. "Dear Dad! Born of a South Indian father and an Irish mother, he showed no external signs of his dark-skinned ancestry, and with his pink skin, electric-blue eyes, and thick, curly auburn hair he could easily, and always did, 'pass' as a white man", de Cruz wrote scathingly.

> This successful exploitation of his external characteristics had taken such deep root in him that he wholeheartedly believed in his own myth: meant "Britain" when he spoke of "home", and sailed serenely into the office toilets labelled "white" instead of using, like humbler but more honest Eurasians, the ones labelled "coloured".[13]

De Cruz rebelled against this attitude. Far from regarding himself as a Eurasian who was superior to Malays, Chinese and Indians, he always felt that he was one of them. At the same time, and in spite of his rejection of his father's views, he thanked God at night in his prayers for living in the British Empire, which he saw as the best of all possible worlds. In spite of his differences with his father, his was an idyllic and playful childhood.

What destroyed the idyll was the Great Depression of the 1930s. Rubber prices crashed, bankrupting hundreds of companies. His father was sacked from his post of chief clerk in the Borneo Company, and his mother, a teacher, took on a second teaching job to keep the family afloat. What was galling was not just that his mother had to work doubly hard, but that this was because his father obstinately refused to accept any job that paid him less than the $250 he had earned a month. He turned down an offer of $200: He was not going to lower his "white man's standards".[14] When his father did find a job in 1935 as a Rubber Restriction Officer in Batu Pahat in Johore — and at $300 a month, which was more than he had earned — the celebrations were cut short by his mother's death from a botched abortion. He recalled his mother asking him one day, not once but twice, whether she would go to heaven. "Of course you'll go to heaven, Mum", he said by way of humouring her. "No one deserves heaven more than you do, after slaving for us all these years." Three days later, she was dead. She was only thirty-four. He blamed his mother's death on his father's stubbornness and intolerable conceit.[15]

When de Cruz was twenty he came across a copy of Jawaharlal Nehru's *An Autobiography*. It shocked him with its insights into the crippling nature of British imperialism. As far as India was concerned, he became anti-British. But India and Singapore were different. Singapore was a beneficiary of British rule. He kept feeling that way until the Japanese walked in, smashing the delusions on which British Singapore had been founded.

De Cruz was a bookworm. At the age of five he was already reading *The Straits Times* from the first page to the last. Wherever he went, he carried a book. One day, when he was about seven, he was walking on the beach and reading when he was hit on the head by a coconut. He fell down unconscious.

The culprits were two boys who were playing cowboys and Indians and throwing little coconuts at each other. They carried him to their home in Sea Avenue and brought him around. The misdirected coconut inaugurated his friendship with Meyer and Saul ("Sonny") Marshall, younger brothers of David Marshall, who would become Singapore's first Chief Minister. From then, he haunted the Marshall family, visiting them after school every evening and over weekends. The younger Marshall brothers stayed very close friends of his until they left for Australia when they were about twenty.

The Marshalls were an extraordinary family, full of life, laughter, intelligence, wit and humour. De Cruz's closeness to the Marshall brothers drew him away from own brothers and other relatives. De Cruz, who was then a proselytizing, crusading Catholic, was determined to convert both the Jewish brothers to Christianity. What occurred, instead, was that they turned him into an atheist!

De Cruz grew up in a depoliticized environment. He did not join any political clubs or movements in school because there were none. However, he and a relative, Leslie Woodford, who was a teacher and scout master, organized a debating society, which the Marshall boys joined. They did not discuss politics, which, among older people, was a word to be feared because it smacked of being anti-British, seen as the greatest crime after being anti-God. So they discussed tame subjects along the lines of "It is better to be a doctor than an architect". Everybody was happy to live under the British. Eurasians had special privileges, being preferred in government service and banks. The white man was their model. They thought that the colonial state of affairs would last forever. They were unaware of what was happening in the outside world and even the news in *The Straits Times* appeared to belong to an alien world. "That world was like a stage on which all kinds of fantastic and stupid and wicked things were happening. But in our little oasis in Singapore, we were safe; we felt secure. And we felt it would go on forever."[16]

It did not. Meanwhile, there were changes in de Cruz's personal life. After having finished school, he was accepted into the Queen's Scholarship class at the elite Raffles Institution. Looking back at those times, he recalled that his sister was born when he was seven. The family physician appeared with a little cradle in his hand and a newborn inside it. He said: "Gerry, look what the Angel Gabriel has brought down from Heaven for you!" Gerry the Pious never questioned that statement till he was fifteen, when he learnt the awful facts of life. They shocked him so badly that he swore to himself that, if he ever had the misfortune to be married, he would treat his wife as his sister! But six months later he was filled with morbid fascination about the subject and rushed to Raffles Library to look for books on it.

He failed to get the Queen's Scholarship and decided to be a journalist. An uncle of his knew A.C. Simmons, who later would become the General Manager of *The Straits Times*. He joined the newspaper in 1940.

The working environment in the newspaper was not political. Everybody was under the spell of British culture, ideas, thoughts, attitudes and values. But he met a person who would prove to be the catalyst in his life. This was a bright young Chinese from Johore Bahru. Billy Kuok Ping Chen had written many letters to *The Straits Times*. When he applied to join its staff, he was accepted because his letters had proved his command of the English language and his intellect. Billy Kuok and de Cruz, both cub reporters, became fast friends and worked in the paper till the Fall of Singapore.

That event was a traumatic experience in de Cruz's life for many reasons.

As I said before, Nehru's *Autobiography* made the first dent, but not an appreciable dent because I was able to compartmentalise it and say, "Well, that's the case with India." But now under my very eyes the British were proving to be completely faithless as I saw it. For example, in that last week in Singapore, coming into town every morning for work at 8 o'clock, we had to undergo a 24-hour round-the-clock bombing by the Japanese. And very often in that six-mile journey from Katong, we had to run and jump out of our buses because the planes would strafe the traffic, you see. We cowered in drains then jumped back into the buses, travelled on a few minutes more and jumped out once more. And all public transport stopped at noon. And you just had to find your own way home. And yet I travelled home in the greatest possible comfort every day! And from the point of view of my father for example — in the most privileged situation — because I was driven home every day by [a] European chauffeur! And who were these European chauffeurs? They were all the officers of the British Army running away from the front line. They had dumped their rifles and their machine-guns and their sub-machine guns and their sten-guns in the Stamford Canal. They had broken into cars lying along the streets, and they were looking for boats to rush away from Singapore. So I would just stop them along the road. Or they would stop beside me and say, "Do you know where we can get boats?" And I would say, "Yes. I'll take you to boats." And I would get in with them and make them take me all the way to Katong. And at the junction of Joo Chiat Road and East Coast Road, I'd point to the sea and say, "You will find your boats there." And they would thank me and they would rush off, and then they'd find rowing-boats. They would jump into them, and they would row out. I don't know what happened to them. But day after day I was brought home by British officers fleeing from the Japanese. That had a terrible impact on me. You see, because we had looked upon the white man as superman. So much of the world was under their power in those days. Eighty per cent of the world they said, was under the British Empire and the rest was divided between the Dutch and the French. And to see them running from the Japanese and finally the eventual surrender of a hundred thousand British soldiers to 30,000 Japanese! Then I knew that something was terribly wrong with the world which I had thought so secure and so safe.[17]

Notes

1. This chapter is based largely on Gerald de Cruz, Oral History Interview, by Foo Kim Leng, Oral History Department, Accession Number 000105/24, Project: Political Developments in Singapore, 1945–65, date transcribed: 12 October 1981, pp. 1–11 (hereafter OHI); and Gerald de Cruz, *Colliding Worlds: Memoirs of a Singapore Maverick* (Singapore: Marshall Cavendish, 2009), pp. 14–30 (hereafter *CW*).
2. Mryna Braga-Blake (ed.), *Singapore Eurasians: Memories and Hopes* (Singapore: Times Editions, published for The Eurasian Association, Singapore, 1992), p. 14.
3. Ibid., p. 17.
4. Ibid., p. 18.
5. Ibid.
6. Joshua de Cruz, Essay, MA World History, Migrants and Minorities in Asia, "'Absent Friends': Eurasian Imperial Subjects in Colonial Singapore", 26 January 2009, p. 1.
7. Ibid., p. 6.
8. Ibid., p. 10.
9. Ibid., p. 12.
10. "Malayan Eurasians", *Syonan Times*, 24 March 2602 [Japanese imperial year], cited in de Cruz, "Absent Friends", pp. 10–11.
11. Ibid., p. 11.
12. Ibid., p. 16.

13. *CW*, p. 72.
14. *CW*, p. 72.
15. *CW*, pp. 73–74.
16. OHI, p. 7.
17. Ibid., pp. 9–10.

Chapter 3

THE JAPANESE OCCUPATION

A week before the British surrendered Singapore to the Japanese on 15 February 1942, Gerald de Cruz, who was working as a reporter for *The Straits Times*, covered the arrival of the last British convoy. Part of it consisted of a group of Sherwood Foresters Anti-Tank Gunners. They looked extremely miserable. He asked one of their officers why. He said that although they were an anti-tank regiment, the ship in the convoy that was carrying anti-tank guns had been diverted around the Cape of Good Hope to the Middle East. So here they were, an anti-tank regiment without anti-tank guns. Although they had handled rifles many years ago, they were being given rifles and sent to the front line. The reality sank into the young reporter: The Far East was expendable, but not the Middle East. So much for Singapore being an Impregnable Fortress.[1] He decided that,

> we cannot depend on other people — white man, black man, yellow man, whoever it might be — to look after us; we must look after ourselves. You see, this is our country and we've got to rule ourselves. And even if we make a mess of it, that's our mess. Because I could see then, when it came to the crunch, we were very low on the list of priorities. Naturally the British

> people had to defend their islands first — first priority; Europe second — second priority; Middle East third — third priority. Far East — far down on the list of priorities.[2]

That moment of realization saw the birth in de Cruz of nationalism and socialism, followed soon after by the need for armed resistance to the Japanese.

> So there was born my nationalism. First, my strong feeling that we'd have to look after ourselves in future and could not depend on anybody to do so. And secondly, my belief in socialism — that the whole of society needed drastic changing and radicalisation, and that capitalism was the economic root of all our evils. And thirdly, stories began filtering through into Singapore that there were Malayan guerillas operating in the jungles; that the Japanese were only free to move around in the towns, but when they left the towns behind them and went into the countryside, they had to be strongly armed and guarded, otherwise the guerillas would attack their convoys and kill them. And I began to hero-worship these guerillas because, whereas the rest of us living in the towns were cowering under the Japanese terror, the terror of the Kempeitei, they were fighting, they were dying for the country. And I saw them as true nationalists and true patriots.[3]

Singapore's Eurasian community bore its part of the burden of the Occupation. When the Japanese came, they asked all Europeans to assemble on the Padang. Those Eurasians who considered themselves Europeans, such as John Eber, duly reported there along with the Europeans. "But a great overwhelming majority of Eurasians who did not pretend to be Europeans remained outside."[4] Where de Cruz's own family was concerned, his brother Guy, who was in the Volunteers, became a prisoner of war. Several cousins were in the Machine-Gun Regiment of the

Volunteer Corp and had fought very bravely in the last stages of the Battle of Singapore. When the Japanese could not be stopped, these Eurasians were told to disband, disperse and reassume their civilian clothing. But the Japanese went around looking for them and eventually managed to pick up most of them. One morning they were marched down Geylang Road to Changi Road. Chancing upon a large group of Eurasians and Chinese who had been in the Machine-Gun Regiment, de Cruz noticed his cousins and spoke to them. They were taken to Yock Eng School and disappeared after that, forever. Rumours went around that they had been machine-gunned to death on the school grounds.

De Cruz himself had served in that Machine-Gun Regiment before the war. But when the war began and the Emergency Regulations were introduced, he was told to leave the Corps because he was in *The Straits Times*. Newspaper staff were categorized as being involved in a vital occupation, among essential occupations such as public services and the provision of water, gas and electricity. So, about a year before the Japanese arrived, he left the Machine-Gun Regiment and became an air-raid warden. Since the Japanese were not looking for air-raid wardens, his life was spared. However, he once had a very narrow escape. Two Japanese soldiers came into his house in East Coast Road. They did not like the colour of his skin and thought that he was a European. One of them went away. From a distance, de Cruz saw him returning with a rifle. He left home and walked all the way to Siglap, where he lived with Sholto La Brooy, the father of his girlfriend at that time. La Brooy had sent his wife and daughters away on a ship. They arrived in India and stayed there for the rest of the Occupation. Since La Brooy's house was almost empty, de Cruz, his father, his grandmother, his brother Dudley and an aunt moved in to keep La Brooy company.

Although La Brooy was double de Cruz's age, they were good friends. "Sholto was the most chivalrous person I had ever known, always ready to give a helping hand to the weak and the frail, especially women and children."[5] And the dead. *Colliding Worlds* relates how, two weeks after the British Surrender, de Cruz and La Brooy were travelling by Kallang Bridge when they came upon a human head, the cheeks bearing signs of torture and the face contorted into a grimace. Next to it was a platform carrying a warning in English that this would be the fate of anti-Japanese elements in Singapore. On the way back, La Brooy disappeared for ten minutes near the bridge. When he rejoined de Cruz, he announced that he had buried the head![6]

De Cruz's memoirs contain a gripping account of how a drunken Japanese officer had charged into the house after having failed to disembowel the family's mongrel because it had barked at him. La Brooy, in his pyjamas, invited the screaming Japanese into the sitting room. The man slashed out at him, as he had done at Bobbie the dog. La Brooy evaded the sword while trying to coax the officer to sit down and make himself at home. He found himself near the door and slipped out of the house. Deprived of his prey, the drunk officer charged into La Brooy's room, which was the only lighted one in the house, and hacked his bed, desk, chair and cupboard into pieces. Only then did he permit himself to be led away by his lieutenant. The next morning the lieutenant drove up in a military car, apologized for the incident, and insisted on compensating La Brooy $600 for his wrecked furniture — in worthless Japanese "banana" currency. De Cruz saw the lieutenant's superior officer, who had almost killed La Brooy, sitting in the back of the car, suffering from a hangover. De Cruz wondered to himself how much that compensation would have been had the Japanese killed La Brooy.[7]

The times were dreadful. The Japanese invasion broke de Cruz's father. According to de Cruz, his father's

> whole world of the white man and the white man's superiority had collapsed even more traumatically than mine because with him it was a deep-rooted thing and part of his religion. And he lost the will to live. He stopped eating and he began withering day after day, day after day. Nothing we could say or do could seem to stop this process. He was literally dying in front of our eyes. Moreover, he was once picked up by the Japanese as part of a group which had been listening to the BBC, which was a grave crime in their eyes. And had been questioned for several days but fortunately was released. But after that, his descent was far, far quicker. And watching him, even though I had been in conflict with him for a long time since my childhood over his attitude towards the local people which was extremely negative, I felt tremendous pity for him and wanted to help him.[8]

Since the death of de Cruz's mother in 1934, his father had concentrated his affection on Hazel, the youngest child in the family. To protect her from the Japanese, she was sent to India along with the La Brooy girls and others. Singapore harbour was being bombed round the clock and their ship was hit, but it stayed afloat because it was very big. It took them to Bombay, from where they went to Delhi. All of them got work with the Americans, in his sister's case with the American Red Cross in Delhi. But although the other girls began to send postcards back through the Swiss Red Cross to Singapore to assure their families that they were all right, no word came from his sister. His father believed that she had died, and this added greatly to his depression. Gerald wondered whether it was possible to get word to Hazel in India if she were alive, and get a message from her. If his father was convinced that she was alive, this might give him a reason for living.

He made contact with a man called Tom Hope, who had worked for *The Straits Times* and had continued working for the *Syonan Shimbun*, as it was called during the Occupation. Hope told him that messages from Indian prisoners of war in Singapore were being sent to India from Radio Saigon, which had come under Japanese control. Therefore, the only way to get a message to his sister was to have it sent from Saigon. But that would be impossible unless he were in Saigon himself. That seemed to be a dead end. However, a few weeks later, Hope told him that the Japanese were looking for news editors for their English-language radio station in Saigon. He applied, along with a hundred others or so. He was one of the eight shortlisted. The other seven backed out by the time of the interview, and he was chosen.

De Cruz was sent to Saigon by train from Singapore. It was a troop carrier. The passengers — he being the only non-Japanese — were herded into cattle trucks. They lived on Japanese privates' rations on the week-long trip from Singapore to Bangkok. There, those going to Saigon were piled into trucks for another week's journey. Finally he found himself in Saigon.

There his path crossed that of an Asian titan. When the Japanese conquered Malaysia and Singapore, thousands of Indian troops who were part of the British forces surrendered to them. The Japanese were planning to attack Burma, and offered them a choice between remaining prisoners of war or volunteering to fight against the British. Many of the Indian officers remained loyal, but others accepted the Japanese offer because they felt for their country, or did not want to rot away in prisoners-of-war camps, or believed that the swiftness of the Japanese victory meant that the British would not be able to hold out in Burma or Australia and so wanted to be on the winning side. The Japanese had brought with them an Indian called Rash Behari Bose, who had been a businessman in Tokyo, to spearhead the

Indian independence movement in Singapore and Malaya and the formation of the Indian National Army (INA). But he had very little stature, particularly in India. The Japanese received a tremendous boost when Subhas Chandra Bose, the leader of the Indian independence movement who was second only to Nehru and Gandhi, arrived in Singapore from Germany, where he then lived. Bose was a remarkable man. Of an ascetic temperament, he was constitutionally unable to sleep for more than two hours a night. He was simple and unassuming and yet very dynamic, with great charisma. His presence as the leader of the Indian independence movement in Southeast Asia gave it vitality and integrity and linked it up with the great movement for India's independence in India itself. De Cruz admired Bose, whom he met several times. Bose, on his part, was taken aback by the fact that de Cruz was a non-Indian participating in the movement for India's independence.

At a personal level, de Cruz discovered in Saigon that messages to India were being sent from another radio station operating from the Radio Saigon premises. This was the Free India Radio Saigon run by INA officers. The second-in-command there was Lieutenant-Colonel Inayet Hassan, with whom he got along very well. Hence, in addition to his work for the Japanese, de Cruz began to broadcast talks on Free India Radio Saigon. He sent a message to his sister telling her that the family was well and asking her to reply urgently because their father was very ill.

While he was waiting for her reply, he got into trouble with the Japanese during the Easter holidays. He assumed that there would be a long weekend, as there was in Singapore, and did not turn up for work till Tuesday. The Japanese were very angry and one of them slapped him. Instinctively, he hit back and knocked the man down. Five Japanese pounced on him and he ran for his life, with them in hot pursuit. Fortunately, they had very short legs and so he was able to out-distance them and run for safety into the nearby office occupied by the staff of Free India Radio Saigon. When the Japanese turned up, the Indians threatened them with a fight if they laid a hand on him. His attackers left meekly, but he ceased to work for the Japanese and joined Free India Radio Saigon full-time.

Hazel replied that she was well. Gerald was very happy, but there was no way of relaying her reply to his father in Singapore. He waited a few months till an INA doctor came down to Singapore. He gave him a message for his father. Later he discovered that the man had never delivered it. Recovering from a bout of malaria, Gerald woke up one morning in Saigon to find his younger brother staring at him. Dudley de Cruz, who had answered an advertisement for a news editor so as to come to Saigon and meet his brother, told him that their father was at the end of his tether. Gerald rushed back to Singapore. Again, the journey took a fortnight. Sadly, his father had passed away a week before he arrived.

Gerald de Cruz's Saigon years — from 1942 to 1944 — left a deep impression on him. Recalling the times in his Oral History Interview, he recounted how the Japanese radio station sent out fabricated news about the war in the Pacific. But Free India Radio Saigon had an entirely different purpose: to send news about Indian prisoners of war and those who had joined the INA and get messages back for them. Also, it worked to increase anti-British feeling in India. Gandhi had refused to ally himself with the Allied forces until India got independence, but the British refused to countenance a transfer of power till after the war because they needed the Indian Army. Free India Radio Saigon supported Gandhi, Nehru and other Congress leaders who were in jail.

Before de Cruz returned to Singapore, the military personnel on Free India Radio Saigon were called to the Burma front. He was made the Director of the station, and remained in that post for several months until he was replaced by civilian Indians from Malaya.

After the war, three of the INA officers with whom de Cruz had worked were tried at the Red Fort in Delhi. Nehru was a part of their defence team. When the British returned to Southeast Asia after the war, a British Intelligence officer of Yugoslav descent named Max Kristac visited de Cruz and told him that "we have enough evidence against you from your broadcast[s] on the Free India Radio Saigon to hang you from seven tiers. But your fate depends on what happen[s] to the INA leaders at that trial." Eventually the British gave up the trial, the prisoners were freed, and nothing happened to de Cruz.

EURASIAN PROGRESSIVE MOVEMENT

De Cruz returned home in 1944. Not long after, American B-20 bombers began to strike Singapore. Thousands came out of their homes to wave at the warplanes, impervious to the danger from the bombs, so great was their hatred of the Japanese. The Japanese responded by making it a crime punishable by death to be seen in the open when Allied bombers were overhead. The irony of the death penalty being imposed for exposure to death could not have been greater.

Caught up in that irony, de Cruz remembered the early days of the Occupation. Thousands of books used to appear on pavements, especially along Rochore Canal Road. These books, looted from European houses and sold for a few cents each, would have a tremendous impact on his life. One was George Bernard

Shaw's *The Intelligent Woman's Guide to Socialism and Capitalism.* The other was *The Mind in the Making* by James Harvey Robinson.

Robinson was the man who finally made de Cruz an atheist. He showed how the human mind had been held in chains in primitive times by magic. After that, it was held in chains by religion. But the age of reason and rationality had dawned and humans had no need to be frightened anymore. They had no need to be blackmailed by the bribe of heaven or the threat of hell. They were able now to reason things out for themselves and to make logic their master, not belief in a terrible, vengeful god watching over them. When de Cruz read that book, he felt truly liberated. Later he realized the irony of being in the middle of a terrible war encircling the world while believing in the supremacy of human reason. Nevertheless, the agnostic process initiated by the Marshall boys had reached its atheistic culmination.

De Cruz's footsteps turned into another road. In Queen Street, where the Malayan Communist Party (MCP) had its office, he found, sitting at a desk and typing, his old friend, Billy Kuok Ping Chen. Kuok provided him news that he brought back to *The Straits Times.* Eventually, that communist news, as it were, led to his expulsion from the newspaper.

De Cruz was happy when the Japanese surrendered in 1945. But the return of the British, he believed, would be temporary. In October 1945, when the Eurasian Association had its first meeting since 1941, he made a forceful speech which argued that the association would have to abandon old attitudes, values and hero-worship of the white man that had been such a strong characteristic of the community. Eurasians would have to see themselves as Eurasians, involve themselves in their country's affairs, and fight for independence. John Eber stood up and supported his views, as did several other young people. But the old people who had run the association felt that the young were being too extreme. That resulted in the formation of a separate Eurasian Progressive Movement, of which de Cruz was chairman and Eber, secretary.

Gerald de Cruz's thinking on being Eurasian in a changing Malaya is revealed by his view of the 1950 Maria Hertogh riots in Singapore, which had been precipitated by a battle for custody of the child between her adoptive Malay family and her Eurasian parents. Writing in *Suara Merdeka*, de Cruz recognized the despair that had overcome the Eurasian community following the riots, in which Eurasians had been victims alongside Europeans. Many Eurasians believed that "there is no place for us in Malaya. The Malays don't want us, and we'll all be slaughtered when and if we get self-government, so let's get out while the going's good." He noted that this was a despairing conclusion because, while individual Eurasians might be able to run away, the overwhelming majority cannot do so. "For good or ill they will have to remain in Malaya and take what comes. It is time that we Eurasians face this fact and begin to ponder over it. If Malaya is our homeland, and it is; and if we have no other place to consider as our 'home', and we haven't, then we have not only the right to be considered as Malayans, we have the duty to take every possible means to make it clear to the other important Malayan communities, that we consider our destiny as Malayans inextricably linked with theirs, and to stop sitting on the fence." De Cruz underlined that fact that it was the imputed association of Eurasians with the white man that had drawn down on them the wrath of Malays. "These riots were the symptoms not only of Muslim anger but of the terrible frustration, political oppression, and anti-British imperialism feelings among the Malays and indeed all sections of the Malayan people. The Eurasians were among the victims because they are still identified with our alien rulers. It is our job then to eradicate such an identification and to help lessen the inevitable communal stresses that are the result of alien rule."[9]

Joe Conceicao, a Eurasian former Member of Parliament and Singapore's envoy to the Soviet Union, recalls with a laugh that de Cruz was a most unusual Eurasian. "In the early 1940s, I saw him a number of times in the Church of the Holy Family in Katong, reading, not the Bible, but Karl Marx!" He adds:

> He was a person with his own mind. He was admired by the community, which was aware of the work that he did [later] with George Thomson at the Political Study Centre. However, the word "communist" is something that Eurasians abhor because most of them are Catholics. There was a groan of regret among Eurasians when he declared himself a communist.

Conceicao concludes: "If there is a legacy, it is that of a rather extraordinary individual. He was an intellectual light. I hope that today's Singapore will throw up multi-dimensional people like him."[10]

Meanwhile, as de Cruz's political thinking matured, Lim Hong Bee and Wu Tien Wang had turned up at his home in Chapel Road to tell him about the idea of forming the Malayan Democratic Union to fight for the cause of a free and, at least, self-governing Malaysia within the Commonwealth.

A new chapter was about to open in de Cruz's life.

Notes

1. Material for this chapter is drawn largely from OHI, pp. 139–59 and pp. 11–23.
2. Ibid., p. 12.

3. Ibid., pp. 12–13.
4. Ibid., p. 139.
5. *CW*, p. 43.
6. *CW*, pp. 45–46.
7. *CW*, pp. 46–47.
8. OHI, p. 14.
9. Gerald de Cruz, "The Maria Hertogh Riots from a Eurasian Point of View", *Suara Merdeka* 2, no. 1 (1951): 11–12.
10. Interview with Joe Conceicao.

Chapter 4

THE COMMUNIST YEARS

The Malayan Communist Party, formed in Singapore in 1930 to establish a Malayan Republic under communist rule, paved the way for an anti-colonial movement in Malaya and Singapore. The MCP's immediate intellectual origins lie at least as far back as the May Fourth movement of 1919, when Chinese students protested against their government's weak response to the way China had been dealt with in the Treaty of Versailles that had ended World War I. The student demonstrations, which were directed also against Japan and the Western powers, broadened into a critique of the feudal past that held the modern Chinese mind in chains. This intellectual and ideological ferment, which reshaped the Kuomintang and gave rise to the Chinese Communist Party, became the "seedtime of the radical tradition" that took root among the Chinese-educated in Singapore and "blossomed forth as the Malayan Communist Party".[1]

However, the MCP was also a local organization, its birth linked to widening nationalist sentiments in Malaya. The legendary Vietnamese leader Ho Chi Minh, who was instrumental in setting up the MCP, was keenly aware that to succeed it would have to act as a genuinely Malayan organization and not an appendage of the Chinese Communist Party. A proletarian revolution could not take place in Malaya without the participation of Malays and Indians, who hardly were likely to be attracted to any party identified closely with China. Acutely conscious of the racial divide in Malaya that would affect proletarian solidarity, Ho advised the leaders of the MCP, dominated by the ethnic Chinese, to learn Malay and reach out to Malays and Indians. Gerald de Cruz's membership of the party is significant in this regard. English-educated and non-Chinese, he was among those members of the intelligentsia who acted as a bridge between the Chinese-educated leadership of the MCP and the wider, multiracial world of Singapore.

The MCP gained significant Chinese support after 1936 by articulating labour discontent and Chinese patriotism stirred by the Sino–Japanese War. Chinese workers, teachers and students alienated from the British colonial order provided the bulk of its largely urban support base although, between 1928 and 1932, it gained a measure of Malay support in Batu Pahat, Muar and the Kuala Pilah district of Negri Sembilan.[2] Atrocities carried out by Imperial Japan, mainly against Chinese and Eurasians during its invasion and occupation of Malaya and Singapore during World War II, solidified the Chinese bases of support for the MCP. Japanese brutalities led the MCP to establish a strong politico-military resistance movement, symbolized by the Malayan People's Anti-Japanese Union and the Malayan People's Anti-Japanese Army. The latter force enabled the MCP to emerge as the strongest social and political movement at the end of the war.[3] C.F. Yong notes that "the Malayan communist movement, despite its vicissitudes in pre-war years, had laid a solid organizational, ideological and membership foundation, without which the party would not have been able to challenge its formidable adversaries, the Japanese until 1945 and the returned British colonial rulers prior to Malayan independence in 1957".[4]

Wartime collaboration between communist guerrillas and the British set the tone for their relations in the immediate post-war years. The MCP was recognized as a legal organization and, indeed, communists were represented on the councils that the British Military Administration set up in major towns. However, de Cruz recalled,[5] they came out into the open only partially. In places such as Kuala Lumpur, Ipoh, Malacca, Penang, Johor and Singapore, they put up little offices where there would be a man who called himself the representative of the MCP, with a small staff working around him. But nobody knew who the party's Secretary-General was or who served on the Central Committee. Party members remained underground by and large, although many front organizations sprang up. In advocating the establishment of a democratic national united front, the MCP's Central Executive Committee said in a document on 5 February 1946 that the programme for such a front should be agreed upon unanimously by all the political parties concerned; that the independence of the various parties should be respected; and that these parties should preserve their right to criticise.[6]

The MCP fell out with the British when it wanted to hold a large demonstration on 15 February 1946 to mark the Fall of Singapore four years earlier and tell its people never to forget the lessons of that day. Thinking that the MCP wanted to commemorate the humiliation of 100,000 British soldiers, who had surrendered to 30,000 Japanese soldiers, the British refused permission for the demonstration. The Communists went ahead, and there were casualties in the confrontation with the police that followed.

De Cruz's sympathies lay with the Communists.

> You see, the fight between the British and the Japanese was a fight between two outsiders. The people of Singapore were

> standing on the sidelines while two foreign armies fought for their position. What the Communists wanted to drive home [was] the lesson — that we must take our own destinies into our own hands. If Singapore is invaded, then the people must fight for it. But they would only fight for it if they were responsible for it. And they would only be responsible for it if they had self-government. Now, the Communist demands at this time politically were not extreme. Ultimately, they wanted a Soviet Republic for Malaya and Singapore which they considered then and now as one unit.[7]

De Cruz was attracted to Communism because of its symbiotic relationship with nationalism. "As the Occupation came to its close I hero-worshipped the Communists.... And I saw them as the best nationalists of all because they were the more disciplined and because they were ready to sacrifice their lives."[8]

MALAYAN COMMUNIST PARTY

The personal and the political were coming together closely now in de Cruz's life. For about six months after the Japanese surrender, he had reported on the Malayan Communist Party for *The Straits Times*. Walking into the MCP headquarters in Queen Street, he had met its representative, Wu Tian Wang. Billy Kuok was his right-hand man. De Cruz's interest in politics did not help him at the paper, which treated the return of the British as the restoration of the status quo ante. The paper wanted to have as little to do as possible with the Communists. De Cruz had several rows with the News Editor, Leslie Hoffman, and was sacked. It was early 1946.

Then, de Cruz's life took a dramatic turn. Lim Hong Bee, whom he had met earlier, invited him to be joint editor of the *Malayan Standard*, a monthly political magazine centred on the need for self-government and the fight against colonialism. It ran articles focused on local issues such as discrimination in the civil service.

One day, de Cruz received a letter from Billy Kuok in Kuala Lumpur. He was starting a weekly English-language newspaper called *The Democrat*, that would work for Malayan independence. He wanted de Cruz to edit it. When he arrived at the paper's office — 59 Klyne Street in Kuala Lumpur — he discovered that it was the headquarters of the MCP's Propaganda Bureau, headed by no less than Chin Peng. Kuok told him that he was starting the paper with some money from his mother, but it was really the party's English-language organ. By now very sympathetic to Communism, de Cruz became its editor. *The Democrat* focused on exposing and denouncing imperialism in Malaya. For example it reported that on a little island called Carey Island, which was full of rubber estates, the management was treating the workers very cruelly. Acting as accusers, prosecutors, jury and judge, the management was imposing fines on the workers and even whipping them. The newspaper also watched British policy very carefully. It criticized the Malayan Union scheme, which the British had introduced on their return to Malaya in 1945 to protect their interests as they prepared the country for eventual independence. The scheme attracted strong opposition, especially from Malays, who saw their political rights being eroded by the extension of citizenship to non-Malays, and was abandoned after barely two years. As for international news, it subscribed to a foreign pro-Communist news agency which gave information on life in the Soviet Union and struggles in China and elsewhere.

Soon de Cruz found that, in addition to his editorial duties, he had become a part of a Communist cell, along with Billy Kuok, an Indian named Jacko Thumboo, and Ah Ming, who looked after the paper's circulation and finances. Osman China

— a Chinese who had been adopted by a Malay family — joined the cell a bit later. Along with a man known to them only as Ah Moke — a Central Committee member who was the cell leader — there were six of them in the cell. De Cruz was put through a stringent education programme for nine months, after which he was admitted into the party formally. He was led up the stairs to a room that was empty except for a table on which there was a lovely tablecloth and a bowl of flowers. "And all the walls were bare except for one wall opposite the table, which was entirely covered by a gigantic Soviet flag, in the centre of which was the hammer and sickle emblem. And we had to raise our right arm in a clenched-fist salute and swear eternal allegiance to the Communist Party. At the same time we were warned that since we were working openly, we should never admit to the fact that we were communists but always call ourselves democrat[s]."[9]

In his memoirs, *My Side of History,* Chin Peng gives a slightly different account of de Cruz's entry into the MCP.

> A local man, de Cruz had an interesting, if unusual, background. During the occupation, he was taken to Saigon and became an announcer on Japanese radio. After the surrender, he returned to Singapore and there made approaches to our headquarters. He said he wanted to work with us. We had a shortage of men who spoke good English. He was very open with us about his collaboration activities and told us exactly how he had been employed by the Japanese. It was Lai Te [Loi Tek] who accepted him into the Party at the end of 1945.[10]

De Cruz discovered the secret of the MCP's strength within the cell organization. Whereas the branch is the basic unit of all other political parties, the MCP went down a step to the cell. Lenin had said that a cell should not have less than three members, because it would then be ineffective, and not more than seven, because then it would be difficult to control. The six members of de Cruz's cell had to meet at least once a week, on Fridays at 3 p.m. In the first part of the meeting, members had to report on how they had carried out orders in the previous week. After each recounted deficiencies in his work, the others would criticize him and point out mistakes that he did not know he had made. Then the cell leader would sum up things.

De Cruz's cell had its hands full. It ran *The Democrat.* It was also the Secretariat. Then, it acted as the liaison between the Central Committee and Malay nationalist leaders such as Burhanuddin Al-helmy, president of the Malay Nationalist Party, Ahmad Boestaman, head of the Malay Youth League, his wife, who headed the Malay Women's Organization, and Musa Ahmad, chairman of the Malay Peasants' Union. Ah Mok explained to de Cruz that they would trust him because he was a Eurasian; they might feel inhibited if the liaison officer were Chinese. Finally, his cell was responsible for the English-language correspondence of the Pan-Malayan Federation of Trade Unions. The once-a-week cell meetings ensured that members did not diverge too far from the party line. "The cell meeting made all of us, as it were, trams, not buses. You know, a tram runs along the line whereas buses are free to go if they wish, wherever they want to go. But the cell meetings kept bringing us back on the party line all the time, advising us, helping us."[11] However, there was much that he found admirable in the work of the cell. His fellow members were not armchair critics, but Communists doing the same work that he did: working for a worldwide movement for freedom, liberation and equality.

> As you began to be subjected to this kind of criticism, real strong bonds of affection developed between the members of the cell, and the cell became in effect your new family. As a Communist you are supposed to give up your family if they were not

> Communist or [were] anti-Communist. Well, the Communists never leave you in a vacuum, the Communist Party. You had to give up one family. But now you get a new family — a family with whom you work, a family with whom you co-operate, a family whom you trust; the kind of family you never had in real life. Because I quickly began to realise that there was one very interesting bond that linked all of us: we all hated our fathers.... I hated my father; I had for many, many years. Ah Ming, the same. Osman China always felt his Chinese family had deserted him by giving him over to the Malays, you see.
>
> And later, I began to discover that many middle-class people joined the party not because they want to win anything.... But the conflict at home between the children, supporting the mother against the father, whenever there's conflict at home between mother and father, the children usually support the mother against the father. But they need their father, you see. The[y] need their father. A child needs both — father and mother. Walk on two legs, as Chairman Mao used to put it in a different context.
>
> And we found in the Communist Party that new father, a kind of father we never had — the understanding father, the all-wise father to guide us on life's journey so to speak.[12]

That, de Cruz recalled, was what the first part of the cell meetings was about. The second part, too, took the form of a report, but in the manner of a confession. Members had to report on their personal sins against party discipline. For example, they were not allowed to watch American and British films because those reflected a capitalist and imperialist view of the world — they were yellow culture — that would weaken and seduce them. But watching Russian or Chinese films was obligatory because they would make them better Communists. If members occasionally watched an American film, as de Cruz did, they were supposed to confess. Also, in a puritan party, members were not supposed to have any relationship with women unless they were Communists as well. Speaking of the "confession", de Cruz took some satisfaction over his role:

> I was very good at this because I had been brought up as a Catholic. And as a Catholic, I'd been taught and trained to go to confession weekly, you see. So I was not ashamed at confessing my sins. But poor Billy Kuok and Ah Ming and Jacko Thumboo! They found it very difficult. They used to stammer and stutter and blush all shades of pinking cream, and they tried to confess their sins. But I got very high marks because I used to make [a] long speech. {Laughter}
>
> Then I began to notice the purpose of this. Because after you've confessed your sins in a Catholic church, you're given absolution by the priest, a priest whom you may not know.... But here, after I'd confessed my sins, Billy Kuok is supposed to criticise me. Because having worked with me and lived with me throughout the week, he would know of any sins, that through shame perhaps or guilt, I might not have confessed, hoping to hide them. Or I might have said something, I might have tried to gloss over my mistakes. So he'll bring it up: "You know Gerry, I'm afraid that's not the point. The point is this, etc etc." And then Jacko would criticise me, and Ah Ming would criticise me, and Osman China would criticise me, then the cell leader would sum up, you see.
>
> So if in the first round of talks our work was being sharpened and made more effective and more pertinent, then in the second, our character was being built. And once again, this had the effect of strengthening the bonds between us as the new family. Because now they knew more about me than my parents ever did. Because we children always keep our sins away from our parents, and very successfully. But here I couldn't. Everything had to be exposed. So I began to feel that I was like a piece of

> clay being moulded and shaped and strengthened by the party for its purposes, in order to achieve its objectives, whatever they were....
>
> [We realized] that our conscience now was in the custody of the party and the party leadership. It was no more a question of right and wrong. It was a question of what is good for the party and what is bad....
>
> And that is how within nine months or a year they can take any ordinary person, and if he becomes a member of the cell, chang[e] him. Outwardly, he's the same. But inwardly, he's a dedicated, fanatical soldier of the Communist Revolution.[13]

De Cruz underlined just how powerful the cell's influence on its members was. Many Communists who left the party came back crawling to their cells one day because of the loneliness outside. "Nobody understands them, nobody accepts them, nobody knows how to criticise them." Also, the bonds within a cell were a resource. "You know, they say that one Japanese can be very stupid but two Japanese are the most intelligent people in the world because they work together. And that's what the Communists have done."[14]

MALAYAN DEMOCRATIC UNION

Yeo Kim Wah notes how the seeds of Malayan nationalism were sown by the British surrender of 1942 and the traumatic experiences that people experienced during the subsequent Japanese Occupation. Aspirations for an independent and united Malaya during the immediate post-war years were represented by the Malayan Democratic Union (MDU), Singapore's first political party and "the pioneer of Malayan nationalism in Singapore".[15] The party was formed in December 1945 by "English-speaking brain-workers", as they called themselves. Christopher Bayly and

Tim Harper describe the MDU's vision of Malaya as an intellectual one, at once inclusive and internationalist, and originating in the urban cosmopolitanism of Singapore. Inspired by a "socialist critique of imperialism", its leaders advanced a programme of nationalization and rural development that would remove non-Malays as middlemen, for it was that British-created role which had created communal tensions in Malaya. The party was set up "at a moment when a broad-based multiracial patriotism seemed to be within reach; an authentic Malayan nationalism that might absorb the various *aliran* of the time". The new mood was evidenced in popular culture. Reflecting the "unstructured and flexible networks of the informal economy", local papers highlighted the close cultural and economic contacts between Chinese and Malays. Growing civic consciousness, that demanded freedom of speech and protection for journalists from harassment, announced the arrival of a stronger sense of the Left — *kiri* in Malay — on the political front.[16] The MDU was a broad church, its character reflected in the fact that the Kuomintang, the Malayan Communist Party, the Eurasian Progressive Association, the New Democratic Youth League and the Singapore Women's Federation were invited to the meeting. "The MDU was an essentially anti-colonial organization which adopted the basic approach that the co-operation of all anti-colonial forces was necessary to achieve the independence of Malaya", Yeo Kim Wah writes. "It viewed the independence movement as one embracing the peasants and the small-holders, the workers and the middle-class. The MDU believed that on its own it could not achieve national independence as it merely represented the middle-class."[17]

The MDU's Manifesto, published on 8 December 1945, declared that the time was appropriate for the formation of a "united representative body which can truly express the real sentiments of the Malayan people". Malaya had been "a political backwater divorced from the march of events in the world", but the stress of World War II and the "terror" of the Japanese Occupation had awakened all the races and classes of the Peninsula to the word "politics".

> Like people in Europe we Malayans realise that life and country cannot be left to chance, but should be intelligently directed to advantage... Democracy is on the march and Malaya must keep up with it. The time has come for Malaya to be free from the standing inhibitions which the traditional concepts of colony impose upon the political, economic and social life of the people.
>
> Malaya has emerged from the storm of the second world war as an active and loyal ally of the United Nations in the fight against Fascism and Japanese Imperialism.... In its dual capacity as a colony and a member of world society, Malaya is particularly fitted to recognise that such wars are inseparably bound up with the doctrine of colonies.

On the basis of these ideas, the MDU presented its programme of demands. It consisted of

- Self-government for Malaya within the British Commonwealth of Nations.
- A Legislative Assembly for Malaya composed of freely elected representatives of the people.
- Votes for all Malayan citizens above the age of twenty-one years, irrespective of race, sex, religion or property.
- Complete freedom of person, speech, press and meeting.
- Educational reform, including free elementary, secondary, and technical education for all.
- A social security scheme, including free medical services throughout Malaya.
- Improved standard of living for all.

- Complete equality in the employment of Malayans and removal of colour-bar restrictions.

The Manifesto went on to detail the importance of the demands. A legislature representing the Malayan people and responsible to them, with the country's governance being placed in the hands of a council of ministers responsible to the legislature, would make it possible for Malaya to be described as a self-governing country. The MDU clarified that it was not asking for Malaya to break away from Britain. "Indeed Malaya with full democratic self government will benefit most if she remains within the British Commonwealth enjoying equality and partnership with the other members of the Empire", the document insisted. As for the four freedoms which it demanded, these were in keeping with the world's great democracies and would enable Malaya to enter "an era of liberty". These were also the four vital freedoms which the United Nations "fought to establish over the forces of Fascism and Japanese Militarism". The MDU promised to guard the liberty of Malayans and "make representation for the abolition of laws which are oppressive in their operation". Education reform demanded that the state educate all men and women to play a responsible part in the shaping of a new Malaya by producing skilled and thinking citizens with a deep knowledge of Malayan affairs and simultaneously international in outlook. Education was a duty of the state and not a privilege which the citizen should pay for. As for social security, no government could call itself efficient if the sick and ailing in health were not assured of the "best and free" medical attention. "This is one of Malaya's greatest needs and it can and must be met." Care for the aged and destitute was a means of remembering those who "in the vigour and strength of their youth played their part in Malaya". The MDU promised to endeavour to introduce old-age schemes and to improve and expand existing pension schemes. To tackle the problem of unemployment, the Manifesto called for a planned economy so that men and women would "fit smoothly into jobs planned for them". The MDU would investigate living conditions and propose concrete measures to achieve a higher standard of living, given that towns and villages "bear witness to the appalling poverty which prevail[s] among the bulk of our population"; in the meanwhile, it supported calls for minimum wage levels. It also called for the total abolition of child labour; a planned economy and social security would make it unnecessary for the children of poor parents to work, which they now were forced to. The document declared its opposition to the colour bar in any form. It ended with a note of support for the proposed Malayan Union, which was "a progressive move towards the consolidation of Malaya". It deplored, however, the proposal to exclude Singapore from the union: Its inclusion was essential for the "existence and well-being of Malaya". The Manifesto ended with looking ahead at "the Malaya of free people".

The MDU faced many obstacles in achieving its goals. It was controlled by the Malayan Communist Party, with the result that British officials and employers were suspicious of radical nationalists, especially those who cooperated with the MCP in an anti-colonial united front. All the same, the MDU contributed to social reform in Singapore and produced a considerable amount of anti-colonial, democratic-socialist literature that influenced later left-wing movements in Malaya. Most important, it formulated a strategy of a nationalist-communist united front to take power from the British, which the People's Action Party utilized later. It was when the MCP took to armed revolution in June 1948 that the political situation turned against the MDU.[18]

Gerald de Cruz joined the MDU and became its Organizing Secretary, acting as a bridge with the MCP. That link was underscored in police files. "Everything that Gerald de CRUZ has done over the last two years and his method of doing it, indicates communist direction", reads an entry from 1948.[19] Another describes him as a "strong and sinister personality".[20] But there is no doubt that he was seen as a key figure of the times. Yet another entry notes how he clarified the MDU's policy at a public lecture given on 15 January 1948.

> It includes the strengthening of the Trade Union Movement, the organisation of peasants into unions; the removal of restrictions on political activities by trade unions and the development of the Co-operative Movement. It also calls for the development of international contacts and the consolidation of a "People's United Front". There is little difference between this policy and the aims of the Communist Party and it lends support to the suspicion that several organisers of political parties and organisations in Malaya are secret agents of the Communist Party.[21]

The MDU fitted in with de Cruz's ideas. The people of Malaya needed to rule themselves and for that one of the first tasks was to raise their level of consciousness. By "the people", he meant the English-educated among whom he moved. Lim Hong Bee and Wu Tien Wang pointed out to him that the Malays and the Chinese had their own parties; the MDU would bring in the English-educated while covering all groups. It would be a truly Malayan type of political organization. For de Cruz, this was the way to go.

Hashimy Tahr, a member of the Malay Nationalist Party (MNP) was elected to the MDU's pro-tem committee. Speaking about this episode, de Cruz said that it revealed the great control that the MCP had exercised over the MDU from the beginning. Hashimy won, although not much was known about his party at that time. The MNP had been formed in late 1945 in Ipoh as a continuation of the radical leftist Malay party, the Kesatuan Melayu Muda (KMM), which had been formed in 1937 by an Indonesian, Ibrahim Yaacob. The KMM was banned in 1940 under the Emergency Regulations that the British had promulgated in Singapore and Malaya following the outbreak of World War II in Europe in September 1939. Many of the KMM's leaders were imprisoned. The Japanese released them when they occupied Singapore. During the Occupation, the KMM maintained contact with both the Japanese, on the one hand, and the MCP and the underground Malayan People's Anti-Japanese Army (MPAJA), on the other.

De Cruz went on to relate how, around August 1945, the Japanese had brought the Indonesian nationalist leaders Sukarno and Hatta to Ipoh as part of their plan to develop a people's resistance movement against the Allies, because they knew that the Allied counter-attack would be coming very soon. The Japanese proposed to Sukarno the formation of Indonesia Raya, consisting of Indonesia, Malaysia, Singapore, Sarawak, Sabah and Brunei. This proposal was welcomed by KMM leaders, who included Ibrahim Yaacob, Burhanuddin Al-Helmy, Ishak bin Haji Mohammed and Ahmad Boestamam. They felt that Malays would have a real future only if they were united as part of Indonesia Raya. But the atom bomb that was dropped on Hiroshima and Nagasaki blew up these plans.

After the Japanese surrendered — but before the British returned — Sukarno paid a secret visit to Malaya to talk to MCP and KMM leaders to persuade them to fight against the British on their return, as he was going to fight against the Dutch. He argued that Indonesians and Malayans would stand a greater chance of success if they fought together against the returning colonialists. The MCP turned him down, arguing that the Labour Party had taken power with a decisive majority in Britain, and Labour had always stood for independence. Hence, the MCP refused to fight. Meanwhile, the KMM wanted to transform itself into the Malay Communist Party, as distinct from the Malayan Communist Party, 95 per cent of whose members were ethnic Chinese. Now, if two Communist parties operated in the same country, it would be bad for the prospects of both. Hence, the MCP said to the KMM leaders that if they had to give themselves a new name in the new circumstances, they should call themselves the Malay Nationalist Party (MNP). This was done.

Thus, the MNP was formed by ardent Malay nationalists like Burhanuddin, Ishak bin Haji Mohammed and Ahmad Boestamam, together with some Malays who had been recruited into the MCP during the war, such as Abdullah C.D. and Rashid Mydin. It was a nationalist party whose nationalist and non-Communist leaders believed in Greater Indonesia, but also in working with the Communists against the British. The nationalist leaders knew that the party had people in its ranks who were actually under the control of the MCP. They accepted this. What was important at the moment was unity; the two streams would separate after independence and fight for popular support.

"So in Singapore, the entry of a Malay Nationalist Party representative into the MDU showed the Communist influence because if the Communists had not suggested it, it would never have happened", de Cruz observed. The Communist objective was also to "promote the idea of Malayanisation of politics in Singapore, which would otherwise be dominated by the Chinese ethnic population majority". The MDU was "the microcosm and the forerunner of what was to become, under Communist guidance, the Pan-Malayan Council of Joint Action".[22]

> The Communists have different stages in their strategy. And as they saw it in Singapore at that time, we were in a liberal,

> democratic, bourgeois stage of the revolution. Now, in that stage therefore, the Communists, as a matter of tactics and strategy, will put forward constitutions that are very, very democratic and seem to be quite moderate. But not as a final aim but only as a stage. Because they know that the people they're going to appeal to are politically still very backward and quite apathetic. If they put anything extreme to them, they'll turn away from it and reject it immediately. So they put forward what seems to be a very nice, reasonable, rational, moderate, democratic constitution. And once we accept that and in the process, every day we are getting more and more politically conscious, then there will be a next stage. At least something a bit more extreme will be put up until they come to us with a dictatorship of the proletariat.[23]

The MDU ran headlong into British plans for Singapore. The British wanted to reinstate the Societies Ordinance, which would give the Registrar almost complete control over all societies, including political organizations. The MDU met in committee and felt that the move should be resisted. The party sent de Cruz and Lim Kean Chye to meet Chan Ming Chen, the Communist representative in Singapore at that time. He was in a difficult position. Although he was the MCP's representative, he needed directives from the Central Committee on a big issue like this. Members of the Central Committee were moving around all the time, as was Loi Tek, the party leader. So Chan said that he would need at least three weeks for a reply and asked the MDU to postpone its decision. But the party felt that it could not. Lim Kean Chye told de Cruz as they walked out of the MCP's office: "Well, at any rate, the MDU has a very strong tail, the Communist Party." But it was the MDU that led the fight against the Societies Ordinance being reinstituted for political parties, and it won without any clear Communist support.

As for the MDU's Malay allies in the Council of Joint Action (CJA) — the most powerful of public organizations in Singapore — these allies, known collectively as the Pusat Tenaga Rakyat, decided to boycott the 1948 elections because British-protected subjects (the subjects of the British-protected Malay States) living in Singapore would not be allowed to vote, whereas British subjects who had been resident in Singapore for a mere six months would have a vote. This discrimination insulted Malays because thousands of them had come to Singapore as British-protected subjects from Johor and other states of the Federation. Though they considered themselves indigenous to the area, they would not be allowed to vote, whereas "an Englishman who seven months ago had been in Hongkong and had been transferred to Singapore, having had six months' residence would be allowed to vote. So they came to us and said: 'We are boycotting and we want you to boycott.'"[24]

Again, the MDU, which at that time was the secretary of the CJA, had to decide its stand on the boycott. Out of a sense of unity with Malays, it decided to boycott the elections. Philip Hoalim, Sr., the chairman of the MDU, held out, arguing that it was a political party, it was a party's job to fight elections, and that, once in the Legislative Assembly, the MDU would have the highest platform in the land to put forward its case and its policy. But he was overruled. The Progressives, led by John Laycock and C.C. Tan, contested the elections and won four out of the six seats. The MDU's boycott strategy succeeded in the sense that only about 25,000 out of the 50,000 people on the electoral roll actually registered. But those 25,000 people voted, bringing in the Progressives and leaving the MDU on the sidelines. The boycott had obviously been a poor decision on the part of the party.

Asked whether the fact that the MDU decided to boycott the elections after the MNP had decided to do so indicated that the

MCP exerted its influence through the MNP indirectly rather than directly on the MDU, de Cruz replied that he had not known this then.

> But since then, I have come to the conclusion that both the MNP and the MCP didn't want us to contest the elections. The way things had been going, if we had contested the elections, we would have won all six seats, and we would have been more deeply involved in the democratic process, and maybe we would grow even further away from the MCP.

The MCP did not tell him directly to vote for a boycott. What he was told was that the MNP was voting for a boycott and that this should be supported.[25]

One interesting aspect of de Cruz's involvement with the boycott is recorded in the files of the Malayan Security Service for March 1948.

> The petition of Gerald de CRUZ on behalf of the MALAYAN DEMOCRATIC UNION to Pandit Nehru, protesting against the participation of Indians in the Singapore Election has angered the local Indians irrespective of their Party affiliations with the exception of a few communists and MDU members. They argue that the MDU have singled out Indians for this insult because they might equally have sent a protest to Chiang Kai Shek.
>
> A large body of Indians are now openly accusing Gerald de CRUZ of being a traitor and in the pay of the Chinese communists. Although the top ranking Indian labour leaders are silent on this subject, a large number of Indian labourers openly criticize de Cruz's action, and some Indian labourers who gathered outside the Municipal Offices on the evening of the 18th March were overheard to apply insulting names to de Cruz and to advocate the assaulting of him when he addressed meetings in future.[26]

COUNCIL OF JOINT ACTION

The MCP set up the Council of Joint Action to create a united front to fight for independence against the British. It would consist of five classes in Malaysia: workers, peasants, the intelligentsia, the petty bourgeoisie, and the national bourgeoisie. The idea was attractive because of the mass support it received from the Pan-Malayan Federation of Trade Unions (PMFTU). The PMFTU accounted for 80 per cent of organized workers across the country. "And the MCP just had to snap its fingers like that, and we had an audience of 20,000 people the next day. All beautifully organised, coming in an eternal procession of lorries to the meeting. So we could put up a very good show."[27] The MCP did not join the CJA directly, but exercised influence through its front organizations — the Malayan Women's Federation, the Malayan Democratic Youth League, the MPAJA Ex-Servicemen's Association and, of course, the Pan-Malayan Federation of Trade Unions — which were open and full members. However, the MCP was always behind the scenes.

Some MDU members, such as Lim Kean Chye, thought that this was wrong and opposed it. One day he took de Cruz with him to discuss the matter with Chan Ming Chen. Chan argued that if the MCP were in it, everybody would say that it was a Communist front organization. Lim argued that if the MCP were out of it, people would have all the more reason for saying that it was pulling the strings. According to Lim, "if you're an open member, then you'll have to accept the decisions we arrive at.... But if you are behind the scenes pulling the strings, then that's more dangerous." But, according to de Cruz, that is exactly what the MCP did, because it wanted to keep its freedom of decision and policy. "It didn't want to make its own policies subject to what the general members might decide. But through its front organisations, of course, the MCP was fully committed to the Council of Joint Action."[28]

In late 1946 the CJA expanded to become the Pan-Malayan Council of Joint Action (PMCJA), later renamed the All-Malayan Council of Joint Action (AMCJA). It rejected all existing Anglo-Malay agreements and demanded recognition as "the *only* body that speaks for all Asiatic communities". The organization was "an attempt to draw together the various *aliran*, or flows of consciousness, within radical politics in Malaya, and all of them, at one time or another, would claim to have been its inspiration".[29] The PMCJA's political platform was based on six principles: a United Malaya, inclusive of Singapore; a fully-elected central legislature for the whole of Malaya; equal political rights for all who regarded Malaya as their real home and the object of their loyalty; the Malay Sultans assuming the position of fully sovereign and constitutional rulers and accepting the advice, not of British "advisers", but of the people through democratic institutions; matters of the Muslim religion and Malay custom being under the control of the Malays; and special attention being paid to the advancement of the Malays.[30]

A tangible expression of these principles was the People's Constitution drafted by John Eber, Kuok Ping Chen, Jacko Thumboo and Gerald de Cruz. It spoke of:

- A united Malaya including Singapore;
- Citizenship that granted equal rights to all who made Malaya their permanent home and the object of their undivided loyalty;
- Melayu to be the title of any proposed citizenship and nationality in Malaya;
- Malay Rulers with real sovereign-power, who were responsible to the people through popularly elected councils;

- A popularly elected central government and popularly elected state councils;
- Malay customs and religion being controlled fully by the Malay people through special councils;
- Special provisions for the advancement of the Malays politically, economically and educationally;
- Malay as the official language;
- A Council of Races set up to block any discriminatory legislation based on ethnicity or religion;
- A national flag and anthem;
- Foreign affairs and defence as the joint responsibility of the government of Malaya and the government of Great Britain;
- Anglo-Malay sovereignty entrenched with the provision of a Conference of Rulers consisting of the Malay rulers and presided over by the British High Commissioner, and 55 per cent reservation of Malay representation in the Federal legislature for the first three terms.[31]

The PMCJA's focus shifted logically from Singapore to Kuala Lumpur to embrace the whole of the country. As executive secretary in Kuala Lumpur, de Cruz became the PMCJA's representative in the public eye. But the public did not know that, behind him, he had the resources of his cell and, indeed, of the MCP. If necessary, he had to swear in public that he was not a Communist. Many believed him. The cover was necessary because he was an open-front Communist, not a card-carrying, underground Communist.

Once again, de Cruz found himself in the midst of political action. His MCP cell leader asked him to go to Malacca and persuade Tan Cheng Lock to lead the PMCJA. Although the Malayan titan was a complete stranger to him, they liked each other immediately. De Cruz stayed with him for three days and heard about his lone struggle for more democracy since 1926.

> And I told him, "You failed, Mr Tan. You failed in the past because you were a lone voice. But as a result of the Japanese Occupation, the masses have awakened. The masses are organised and the masses are waiting for leadership, the leadership that only you can give. So why don't you join us now?
>
> And he agreed to. At the end of three days and three nights, he agreed to become President of the Pan-Malayan Council of Joint Action. And he served as President right up to the outbreak of the insurgency when it was dissolved. He was a very good President. He let us have our way. He never interfered. He listened to all the arguments, and if he had some comments, he would make them.[32]

De Cruz was impressed by Tan. He was learned, and had studied Kant and Marx. He called himself a socialist, although this was because he seemed to think that sitting down and having lunch with rubber tappers when he visited his rubber estates made him a socialist. He had a very low opinion of British colonial administration. He took de Cruz through the length of his home in Malacca. On the walls he had pictures of all the colonial governors with whom he had been associated since 1926. Caustically, he dismissed one man as a fool, another as a donkey, yet another as an idiot, and another as a coward.

Although Tan Cheng Lock accepted all the proposals brought forward in the PMCJA, he felt that the council should give its work more urgency because the British were ignoring it. "They had UMNO with them. They were in secret counsel with UMNO for a new Constitution." So Tan decided to organize a *hartal* — a general strike — in Malacca. "And Malacca died for that day." When the MCP saw how effective the technique could be, it organized the next one in Perak — through de Cruz in the council's name. "And Perak died for one whole day."[33] And then a pan-Malayan *hartal* was organized from Penang to Singapore.

The *hartal* had originated in India, where Mahatma Gandhi had used it in his fight against British rule. Tan Cheng Lock, one of the Chinese on the Japanese blacklist, had spent the Japanese Occupation years in India to avoid being beheaded. In India he had become a great admirer of the Indian National Congress and of its methods. He learned about the *hartal* and decided to use it in Malaya. According to an intelligence report, it was on 19 July 1947 that the first suggestion was made of the adoption of Indian methods of fighting the Constitution. "In a speech to the MDU GERALD DE CRUZ stated that he and TAN CHENG LOCK would lead a Civil Disobedience Campaign and would be 'prepared to go to gaol, for Political Prisoners of today are likely to be the Prime Ministers of tomorrow'. He added that as the PMFTU and the workers were in support of the PMCJA/PUTERA proposals a one-day general strike might be arranged."[34]

Of course, the popular response to the Malayan *hartals* was overwhelming. However, even at that time de Cruz felt that a *hartal* was strategically not really helpful. It angered the British, but things went back to normal because there was no follow-up plan to put cumulative pressure on the government. And even if there had been such a plan, there were no resources to put it into effect. "People were prepared to stop work and have a holiday for one day — an unofficial holiday. And that was a lot from our point of view. But from the government's point of view, it was just one day in the year."[35]

Another mistake was about to be made. When the government appointed a Consultative Committee in December 1946 to listen to criticism of the Malayan Union plan and propose amendments to it, the PMCJA boycotted it. Admittedly, to de Cruz, it was right for the council to question the credentials of people on the committee, for they had been nominated by the British. Also, the PMCJA produced its rival People's Constitution. But de Cruz thought that members of the PMCJA acted like very green politicians, because the PMCJA had forfeited a chance to state its case at the highest level allowed by the government. Its views would have been widely reported in the newspapers and its case would have been carried a step further. But because of an "adolescent" boycott, like its previous boycott of the 1946 election, it missed a golden opportunity to explain itself to the people.[36]

Nevertheless, de Cruz enjoyed the political work that he was doing in the PMCJA. Ceremonies were held in villages and towns, where the people's flag would be raised and the People's Constitution explained. These meetings had a festival-like character. For example, the Communists used songs to sway hearts. They made a love song in which a boy and a girl sat and talked in a garden. Then she began to sing. "Oh darling", she said, "let's stop talking about ourselves and talk about the fate of our country. I have heard something about the People's Constitution. Can you explain to me what it is about?" The boy explained it to her — in verse.

These were large gatherings. When de Cruz read later that Winston Churchill had addressed perhaps the biggest audience of his career — consisting of nearly 20,000 people — he was surprised because this was the normal size of a meeting in Malaya, which was experiencing politics for the first time. "Of course, afterwards I realised that when you've had too much politics, you get a bit bored with it. But to us, politics was a new thing." Behind the meetings were the organizing abilities and influence of the Communists. "It was not the Council of Joint Action as such, which was able to bring the masses, attract the masses. It was the Communist organisation and discipline which brought people to the meetings." These would be organized in Bahasa Melayu (Malay), Chinese and English, with Tamil added if many Indians attended them.[37]

All in all, de Cruz's job was to carry out decisions taken at PMCJA meetings. He also had to keep its members together. He worked hard to develop good relations, particularly with the Malay leaders. The MCP was quite confident of the non-Malay leaders, while Tan Cheng Lock and his people looked after the right-wing leaders. De Cruz reached out to the Malays.

In his memoirs, Ahmad Boestamam says that de Cruz's ability to speak in Malay at public meetings made him extremely popular among left-inclined Malays throughout the country, "until if a public meeting were held which he could not attend people would be sure to ask us: 'Where's de Cruz? Why hasn't he come' and so on.... Thunderous applause was inevitably given him whenever he made a speech before them." De Cruz was enthusiastic about visiting Malay villages, sleeping on the floor in houses there wearing a sarong, relishing Malay food and eating with his hands just as Malays did, occasionally wearing a *songkok*. Boestamam concludes: "I have purposely written at length about de Cruz as I want to put a question to present day goodwill leaders among the non-Malays, in this fashion: 'Who among you is able actually to practice goodwill, as was done by de Cruz..., not just theorize?' "[38]

According to de Cruz, the MCP never regretted having allowed the MDU to take the lead in the CJA while remaining in the background. One reason was that the MCP had so many members in the MDU that it was confident of being able to stifle anti-MCP reactions within it and control it ultimately. The other reason was that the Communists wanted a stool pigeon to take the brunt of the blame in case anything went wrong. This was a part of the MCP's strategy of having a legal arm and an illegal arm working simultaneously. An illegal arm was necessary for doing many things that the legal arm would not be able to approve of.

On balance, to de Cruz, the MDU had captured the imagination of the English-educated, but it began to lose its influence after it boycotted the elections of 1948 and new political parties were formed. Then, in June 1948, the British clamped down the Emergency Regulations and banned the Pan-Malayan Federation of Trade Unions, the Malay Nationalist Party and the Malayan Communist Party. The MDU decided at a Central Committee meeting to disband itself, arguing that this was necessary to protect its members. The pro-Communists and the Communists on the Central Committee accepted that the situation had gone too far once the Emergency had been proclaimed and a state of war existed between the Communists and the government. The non-Communists on the committee were frightened that they might be jailed because of their association with the Communists in the MDU. Some members of the MDU joined the Singapore Anti-British League and met to discuss Marxism. They also began secretly writing for the English-language edition of *Freedom News*, the Communist underground newspaper, and distributing it clandestinely in Singapore. An Intelligence report comments:

> The Malayan Democratic Union announced its dissolution on June 24th ostensibly on the grounds that it could no longer serve any useful purpose after the introduction of Emergency Regulations. The MDU had in any case come to a political impasse and it is likely that the final decision was hastened by the publication in the MCP REVIEW of the MCP withdrawal of support for the so-called People's Constitution which was largely a product of the MDU as secretarial organisation of the AMCJA/PUTERA group.

Information from secret sources indicated, the report adds, that "in the MDU the only actual members of the MCP were P C KWOK and Gerald de CRUZ. The former has disappeared from his normal haunts. The latter is still in Singapore and is believed to be intending to start a reading circle among the Katong members of the MDU."[39] Another report says that he "is expecting to be arrested under the Emergency Regulations".[40]

Was Gerald de Cruz the Communist a threat to the British Empire? Leon Comber knew de Cruz socially from 1946 to 1948, when he was in the Special Branch in Kuala Lumpur, and later in Johor, when he headed the Special Branch in the state. De Cruz was associated more closely with Comber's wife, the illustrious writer and doctor Han Suyin, than with the British Intelligence official. "They were both Eurasian, to start with. There was a common bond there. They were also both Left-wing", Comber says. Now a Senior Visiting Fellow at the Institute of Southeast Asian Studies, he adds:

> He would be likely to have a Special Branch file, which I have never seen, which would be opened on people who are likely to be anti-Establishment. That does not mean that they are going to be a threat but, in those days, going to be Left-wing and opposed to the capitalism of the imperial system which was in force here and the way in which the colonial government looked at anti-colonialism as a threat. But he would not have achieved a position to constitute a threat. He'd be a supporter, but he was not a leader or thought of as a leader.... They [the Communists] would use him from time to time if they wanted to, and he wanted to as well. That's not to say he's to be dismissed.... His knowledge of Malay was above-ordinary. He could use Malay as a political tool. You must have a very good knowledge of any language if you are going to do that.... He could be used in many ways because his English was so extremely good, but

> not beyond that. The MCP did not want Eurasians as leaders in what was a Chinese movement, and the Chinese are never going to accept a non-Chinese as a leader of a Chinese movement.[41]

According to Comber, de Cruz "was an idealist". "Gerald was an intellectual. He impressed me to no end because he was so articulate. I used to listen to him, I wouldn't say entranced but with interest." What intrigued Comber was that "Gerald transmogrified himself from a Roman Catholic Eurasian to seemingly a supporter of Japanese rule." Then he "seemingly converted to communism". Then "he went over to the government side", and later he converted to Islam. Comber finds problematic de Cruz's earlier support for Japanese imperialism, which, while hostile to Western colonialism, was no less global in its ambitions. Comber points out that the Japanese idea of a Greater East Asia Co-Prosperity Sphere was not limited to Southeast Asia, but was meant to be extended to Australia, the Pacific Ocean, and possibly south New Zealand, and meet up perhaps with the Axis spheres of Germany and Italy in the Middle East. "But there was Gerald there, working with the Japanese happily in Saigon." De Cruz used his "English English" as a tool for Japanese propaganda. However, Comber concludes by underlining again that de Cruz's idealism survived these changing phases of his life intact.

THE RIFT WITH COMMUNISM

When de Cruz heard that *The Democrat* was to be folded up, no reasons were given. The real reason was, of course, that Loi Tek had run away with the party's funds.

De Cruz's cell leader, Ah Moke, told him the story of Loi Tek, the triple agent who had worked for the French, the British and the Japanese while pretending to be a Communist and had, indeed, reached the top of the party. He had been discovered when the MCP had hosted a tea reception for a Vietminh delegation visiting its office in Singapore. These were Vietnamese who had worked in Singapore, had gone home for a holiday after the war, and were now back. A member of the delegation asked Chin Peng: "Who is that chap there standing in the corner?" Chin Peng whispered that it was the party's Secretary-General, Loi Tek, and wondered why he had asked. The Vietnamese said that he had often been noticed in the company of the Head of the Japanese Kempeitai at the Southern Hotel in Cross Street. The MCP appointed Chin Peng to investigate the matter. Chin Peng discovered that Loi Tek had been working for the Japanese throughout the Occupation.

Immediately, the MCP found an answer to many mysteries during that period. For example, there was the infamous incident of 1 September 1942 in which the party had called a special meeting at Batu Caves to plan a resistance movement. The Japanese, who had been tipped off, surrounded the area and attacked the Communists. Only a few of the leading cadres attending the meeting managed to escape; the rest were killed. Loi Tek had betrayed his comrades.

When Loi Tek heard about Chin Peng's investigation, he disappeared with the party funds: nearly a million dollars. The MCP grew so short of money that its representatives in various towns had to sell their cars.

De Cruz was so shocked that he began to have concerns about who might be working for the British in his time in an authoritarian party in which the cells had no knowledge of how the top leadership operated.

However, beyond personal doubts, what caused de Cruz's rift with the MCP was its decision to launch an armed struggle in 1948. Chin Peng, who was the leader by then, wanted to have a bash at the British because, having been outmanoeuvred by the

British and UMNO, the MCP was not winning on the political front. However, de Cruz had very strong reservations. These had to do with the fact that the order for the Communists to go into armed revolt had come from the Soviet Union. He began to re-examine his ideological affiliations because he felt that it was wrong for Moscow to use the MCP as a pawn in whatever games it was playing. He had always seen the Communists as patriots. Yet, here they were now, willing to organize a civil war, "the worst of all wars, brother against brother so to speak, killing of our own Malaysian people at the behest of orders from a country 8,000 miles away or so".[42]

De Cruz's reservations about the MCP reflected the tensions and distrust created by the Cold War. The Grand Alliance among the United States, the Soviet Union and Great Britain had broken down after World War II. President Harry Truman declared in March 1947 that the United States would "provide political, military and economic assistance to all democratic nations under threat from external or internal authoritarian forces". In June 1947, U.S. Secretary of State George C. Marshall proposed the extension of massive economic assistance to the nations of Europe devastated by war.[43] The Truman Doctrine and the Marshall Plan were seen as a part of American efforts to contain the Soviet Union, which had carved out a sphere of influence in Eastern Europe. The case for containment was made in an article, "The Sources of Soviet Conduct", authored anonymously under the name "X", by the American diplomat George Kennan in the 1947 issue of the American journal, *Foreign Affairs*. Noting that the political nature of the Soviet Union was such that it could not coexist with capitalist nations, he called for patient but firm containment of the communist state. Two months after Kennan's article was published, Soviet Politburo member and Leningrad party chief Andrei Zhdanov delivered a report to the secret inaugural conference of the Cominform, the international communist information bureau, in the Polish town of Szklarska Poremba. Mirroring Kennan, Zhdanov emphasized the ideological differences between the Soviet Union and the United States and believed that confrontation between them was inevitable. The 25 September 1947 declaration, which came to be known as the Zhdanov Line, described the world as being divided irreconcilably between two ideological camps.

Zhdanov's Two Camp thesis declared:

> A new alignment of political forces has arisen. The more the war recedes into the past, the more distinct become two major trends in post-war international policy, corresponding to the division of the political forces operating in the international arena into two major camps: the imperialist and anti-democratic camp, on the one hand, and the anti-imperialist and democratic camp, on the other. The principal driving force of the imperialist camp is the U.S.A. Allied with it are Great Britain and France.... The imperialist camp is also supported by colony-owning countries, such as Belgium and Holland, by countries with reactionary anti-democratic regimes, such as Turkey and Greece, and by countries politically and economically dependent on the United States, such as Near-Eastern and South American countries and China.
>
> The cardinal purpose of the imperialist camp is to strengthen imperialism, to hatch a new imperialist war, to combat socialism and democracy, and to support reactionary and anti-democratic pro-fascist regimes and movements everywhere. The anti-imperialist and anti-fascist forces comprise the second camp. This camp is based on The U.S.S.R. and the new democracies [of Eastern Europe]. It also includes countries that have broken with imperialism and have firmly set foot on the path of democratic development, such as Rumania, Hungary and Finland. Indonesia and Vietnam are associated with it; it has the sympathy of India, Egypt and Syria. The anti-imperialist

> camp is backed by the labour and democratic movement and by the fraternal Communist parties in all countries, by the fighters for national liberation in the colonies and dependencies, by all progressive and democratic forces in every country. The purpose of this camp is to resist the threat of new wars and imperialist expansion, to strengthen democracy and to extirpate the vestiges of fascism.[44]

The appearance of the Zhdanov Line galvanized communist parties around the world. For those in capitalist, colonial and semi-colonial states, it suggested that they should break with united front tactics, in which they cooperated tactically with non-communist forces in the struggle against colonialism, and adopt the strategy of armed struggle. Two leading communist organizations, the Budapest-headquartered World Federation of Democratic Youth and the Prague-based International Union of Students, had initiated an anti-colonial campaign when the Kremlin had given its support to the Indonesian liberation movement in 1946. That campaign, buoyed by the Zhdanov Line, culminated in the Conference of Youth and Students of Southeast Asia Fighting for Freedom and Independence, held in Calcutta from 19 to 26 February 1948. The Calcutta conference was attended by delegations from Burma, China, Ceylon, India, Indonesia, Malaya, Nepal, Pakistan, the Philippines, the Soviet Union and Vietnam. Malaya was represented by Lee Song, who, although he was not a high-ranking MCP leader, was sent as delegate because of his skills in English. Immediately after the conference, and also in Calcutta, the Communist Party of India held its second congress from 28 February to 6 March.

The traditional view is that the Soviet delegates at the conference passed on the Cominform's instructions to their Southeast Asian counterparts to embark on armed struggle. Indeed, insurrections broke out almost simultaneously in Burma,

Indonesia, Malaya and the Philippines. The Burmese Communist Party took up arms against its erstwhile comrades in the Anti-Fascist People's Freedom League after the British governor had appointed non-communist AFPFL leaders to the country's executive council. In Indonesia in September 1948, the PKI took control of Madiun and its leader, Muso, declared a new republican government. Communists overran other towns in East Java as well, killing religious leaders. President Sukarno instructed the military to crush the rebellion. Muso was killed in the consequent assault on Madiun, led by the Siliwangi Division. Over in the Philippines, the Huk insurrection peaked in 1950 and was brought under control only gradually over the next five years. In Malaya, the murder of three European planters in the Sungei Siput area of Perak state on 16 June 1948, initiated the imposition of the Malayan Emergency, which lasted from 1948 to 1960.

Did the Cominform inspire these acts of violence through the Calcutta Conference, or were the insurrections the result of local conditions? Local conditions varied so much across Southeast Asia that it is difficult to believe that these communist parties acted spontaneously, and at about the same time, solely on the belief that their countries were ripe for armed revolution. However, Larisa Efimova, a specialist in Soviet–Indonesian relations, provided the contrary argument. She consulted previously closed archival documents of the Central Committee of the All-Union Communist Party (of Bolsheviks) [CC AUCP (B)], the All-Union Leninist Young Communist League, or Komsomol, and the Anti-Fascist Committee of Soviet Youth. She concluded that while "the Soviet leadership instigated the anti-colonial and anti-imperialist ardour on the part of the Soviet and the world communist-oriented youth in their propaganda activity ... the CC AUCP (B) strongly rejected all practical efforts of the Soviet youth leaders to put these slogans into practice". Indeed, the Soviet leadership "harshly criticised the youth activists who took seriously the propaganda rhetoric and tried to realise it".[45]

In this vein, Lim Hong Bee's autobiography, *Born into War*, disagrees with such accounts of Soviet backing of the MCP's "alleged attempt to set up a 'Red Republic of Malaya'". He argues that the "so-called 'hard evidence'" of this attempt was a telegram sent by the MCP's Singapore City Committee to Stalin congratulating him on the twenty-ninth anniversary of the October revolution.

> It was also alleged that the Comintern had issued an edict ordering an insurrection in Malaya! The existence of the telegram, though probably true, would hardly be admissible as evidence in any civilised court of law. The telegram had been sent openly at normal post office rate through the Singapore General Post Office — hardly the procedure for a revolutionary conspiracy!

As for the alleged "Comintern" directive to start a Malayan Communist insurrection, Lim finds the credibility "even more insupportable". He notes that Dennis Bloodworth, in his book, *The Tiger and the Trojan Horse*, claims that the Comintern, through Zhdanov, had instructed the MCP to start the insurrection. "How does he know?" Lim asks sternly. He argues that "not even the bug-eyed scrutineers of the Malayan Special Branch can proffer even a faintly acceptable fingerprint — or toe-print for that matter" of Zhdanov. "In any case the Comintern had been dissolved in 1941 — five years prior to the alleged directive!"[46]

Efimova's analysis has been criticized on the grounds that she did not have access to the papers of the party's higher echelons, where any proof of a new militant line on Southeast Asia would likely to be found rather than in the documents that she consulted. However, on the present state of archival knowledge, it would be reasonable to suppose that although Moscow had not issued any directive for armed action at Calcutta, the intent and tenor of Zhdanov's two-camp proclamation was clear enough to provide the operative framework for the outbreak of insurrections in Southeast Asia. Karl Hack adopts this approach, arguing that direct instructions from the Kremlin were neither given nor required, because the ideological climate created by the Zhdanov Line was sufficient evidence to Asian Communists of the need to adopt a new, aggressive approach. Many local cadres took up that line enthusiastically and used it in their debates.[47]

De Cruz was inclined to support the conspiracy theory. His anger over the MCP's new insurrectionary line after the Calcutta Conferences is clear:

> On their return, these greater details are discussed at Central Committee level. And if the Party leader disagrees, then he's guilty of a grave offence because the Soviet Communist Party or the Soviet Union is seen as the headquarters of Communism. And so our primary duty as a Communist — it's not to preserve the integrity of our country but of the Soviet Union, you see, because our global aim and ultimate aim is Communism throughout the world. But [if] there's no Communism in Malaya, that doesn't matter so much. But if Communism is defeated in the Soviet Union, then, from the point of view of the Communists, that is absolutely catastrophic. So, priority number one is obeying the orders and the needs of Soviet foreign policy as enunciated by Soviet leaders. And that is what was done in this case.[48]

De Cruz said that he first came to know of the MCP's decision to resort to armed struggle when its delegates returned from the Calcutta Conferences in early 1948. His cell leader said to him:

> We have a plan. Although the conditions for armed revolt laid down by Lenin are not at present in existence — economic chaos

> in the country, complete loss of confidence in the government, equality, at least equality of forces between the government and the Communists ... we are going to create those conditions.
>
> For example ... we have been too soft where strikes are concerned. Now we are going to call strikes not locally but nationally. We are going to call all the rubber workers throughout the Federation [to go] on strike. We are going to put impossible demands so that the employers or the estate owners cannot meet our demands. After that strike has been well established, we're going to call out all the tin-miners on strike. When that strike is well-established, we're going to call out all the transport workers on strike. Then all the dock workers on strike, so that economic chaos will be created, the people's confidence in the government will be lost.
>
> Now, we know our weak points. The weak point is among the Malay peasants. So we've chosen the three or four greatest areas of Malay concentration, Malay peasants' concentration, and we will be sending in our trained propagandists in the Malay language to attack them and soften them up. And then when the time comes, we are going into the jungle.

Of course, the British slapped down the Emergency Regulations before this plan could take off.[49] Nevertheless, the MCP's strategy of armed revolt drew on to hapless civilians the wrathful repression and cruel excesses of the Malayan Emergency that lasted from 1948 to 1960.

So strong were de Cruz's feelings against the insurrection that, as late as 1971, he would engage Michael Stenson in a vigorous debate over the proper interpretation of the 1948 revolt. Was it part of a general Communist revolt in Southeast Asia, or was it the result of specific, concrete, local conditions that compelled the MCP to act so as not to lose its political position? Stenson argued that the internal Malayan situation had forced the MCP to choose revolt. He noted that the MCP's policy between

August 1945 and early 1948 had rested on the formation of a peaceful united front with the object of achieving a "more or less constitutional takeover of power".

> The policy was predicated upon British acceptance of open political, trade union and similar activities which would be considered legal in Britain itself. It was no doubt partially predicated upon the MCP's retention of a significant administrative-cum-intimidatory power. I would argue that it was only when it became apparent that both major avenues of expression, political and trade union, administrative-cum-intimidatory, were almost completely to be denied to militant left-wing groups that the MCP decided to reverse its previous policy.[50]

As for the contention that it was policy directives from abroad that had made the MCP act, Stenson preferred to emphasize, instead, the atmosphere of "rising international militancy which was both necessary, because of capitalist aggression, and propitious, because 'democratic' forces, such as those in China and Vietnam, were on the offensive". He added, "The MCP seems to have been generally receptive to the international 'message' because it fitted in with Malayan facts. The only alternative to much more decisive action in 1948 was governmental elimination or erosion of most of the organisational and other gains made by the Party since 1941."[51]

In his rejoinder, de Cruz did not deny that the British had tried to put severe restrictions on the MCP. But he stuck to his argument that the revolt broke out in the same year that saw revolts in other parts of Southeast Asia; this provided "overwhelming circumstantial evidence" that it was part of a concerted Communist uprising heralded by Zhdanov's new hard line.[52] Indeed, so desperately did Stalin need to divert American attention from his planned coups in Eastern Europe, that in countries such as India, Burma and Indonesia, he ordered the communist parties "to revolt against their own national and nationalist leadership".[53] De Cruz remembered what his cell leader had told him at the time. He had said that conditions had to be created to destroy confidence in the British administration and to undermine the efficiency and order of their rule. This would be done by sowing economic chaos.[54] Consequently, he predicted,

> police and workers would clash up and down the peninsula; ships would lie at anchor rotting in the harbours; Singapore and the other ports would die; and gloom and despair would envelop the country.
>
> "Then we shall go into the jungle and raise the banner of revolt," he said, "and ask the people to support us against British imperialism as once they supported us against Japanese fascism."[55]

The "swift and ruthless" British reaction to this strategy turned it on its head. "In effect, the British forced the MCP into the jungle before it could put its plan of wrecking the economy and sabotaging the morale of the people and the government into action."[56]

Nationalism had brought de Cruz to communism; it was nationalism again that drew him away from it. But he remained steadfast in his support for Malayan independence. *Facing Facts in Malaya,* a pamphlet published in 1952, states the case for Malayan nationalism with a moral fury and a polemical calm befitting a man who had been a communist once. The tract denounces the vendetta being waged by the vindictive Gerald Templer administration against civilians during the Emergency. De Cruz recalls the heroic exploits of anti-Japanese guerrillas in the jungles, and relates that moment in Malayan history to the awakening of the people of Malaya. He excoriates British rule for prolonging the dreadful misery of the Malay peasantry. This is vintage Gerald de Cruz, the man who could not countenance an injustice done to one human without witnessing in it an injury to the entire human race. This is the de Cruz who was led to communism by his belief that every individual is implicated in the fate of the world; to pretend otherwise is to rationalize away the truth. He takes a long view of time.

> British rule has not stimulated a Malayan consciousness or the need for a Malayan nationality; it is the contrary that is true. Educationally, politically, economically and culturally, British rule has kept the various communities in their respective places; and it was not till the world broke ruthlessly through this isolation, in the shape of the predatory and terrorising Japanese invasion and occupation, that these artificial barriers between the communities collapsed for ever.[57]

The times had changed irrevocably: It was necessary now for the political structure, too, to change.

> We need a Government firmly based on the rank and file Malayan, capable of seeing him, not in his historical role as a hewer of wood and drawer of water, but, as the swiftly unfolding scenes all around him in Asia bear witness, in the light of what he can become and is becoming — a man conscious of his dignity, standing on his own feet, and carving out his own destiny.[58]

Looking back at 1948, de Cruz recalls that the MCP wanted him to run *Freedom News* from the underground. He told Ah Moke that he was not ready. Ah Moke agreed to give him time to settle his affairs in Singapore, where he would have a contact man who would tell him how to join the party in the jungle. Every Friday, de Cruz would go to a bicycle shop in Jalan Besar and spend an hour with the man, ostensibly to help him with his English. This de Cruz did by teaching him out of *Soviet Communism: A New Civilisation*, a book by Sidney and Beatrice Webb. But one day, when he arrived at the shop, the owner told him that the man had been picked up by the police the previous day at Middle Road. So his contact was broken.

It was in the circumstances of his break with the MCP that de Cruz took the most remarkable, most improbable, and perhaps the most irresponsible of decisions in his life: to work his way to the Soviet Union to find out what was happening!

Notes

1. Edwin Lee, *Singapore: The Unexpected Nation* (Singapore: Institute of Southeast Asian Studies, 2008), p. 33.
2. Yeo Kim Wah, *Political Development in Singapore 1945–1955* (Singapore: Singapore University Press, 1973), pp. 173–74.
3. Cheah Book Kheng, *Red Star over Malaya: Resistance and Social Conflict during and after the Japanese Occupation of Malaya, 1941–1946* (Singapore: Singapore University Press, 3rd ed., 2003), pp. 54–56.
4. C.F. Yong, *The Origins of Malayan Communism* (Singapore: South Seas Society, 1997), p. 278.
5. Material for this chapter is drawn substantially from OHI, pp. 21–77 and pp. 153–203.
6. MCP Central Executive Committee, "The Malayan Communist Party's Exhortation to all the Malayan Compatriots for the Implementation of the Democratic Program", 5 February 1946.
7. OHI, p. 170.
8. Ibid., p. 174.
9. Ibid., p. 162.
10. Chin Peng, *My Side of History — As told to Ian Ward and Norma Miraflor* (Singapore: Media Masters, 2003), p. 192.
11. OHI, p. 164.
12. Ibid., pp. 165–66.

13. Ibid, pp. 166–68.
14. Ibid., p. 47.
15. Yeo, *Political Development in Singapore,* op. cit., p. 279.
16. Christopher Bayly and Tim Harper, *Forgotten Wars: The End of Britain's Asian Empire* (London: Allen Lane, 2007, pp. 200–202. *Aliran* means "stream" in Malay.
17. Yeo, *Political Development in Singapore,* op. cit., p. 89.
18. Yeo, *Political Development in Singapore,* op. cit., p. 279.
19. Malayan Security Service, Political Intelligence Journal No. 4 of 1948, 29 February 1948. CO 537/3751 1948.
20. Memo by O.H. Morris, Principal of the Colonial Office, London, dated 6 May 1948, attached as a commentary to the main file: Malayan Security Service, Political Intelligence Journal No. 9 of 1948, 15 May 1948. CO 537/3751 1948.
21. Malayan Security Service, Political Intelligence Journal No. 2 of 1948.
22. OHI, p. 34.
23. OHI, p. 26.
24. OHI, p. 173.
25. OHI, p. 62.
26. Malayan Security Service, Political Intelligence Journal No. 6 of 1948, 31 March 1948. CO 537/3751 1948.
27. OHI, p. 63.
28. OHI, p. 63.
29. Bayly and Harper, *Forgotten Wars,* op. cit., p. 363. When the MNP was accused of having sold out Malays, it withdrew from the council to set up a parallel coalition, the Pusat Tenaga Rakyat (PUTERA), or Centre of People's Power. Co-operation soon followed in what was called the AMCJA-PUTERA, but the coalition was one of contradictory interests because "PUTERA stood for a *Melayu* nationality, and the AMCJA's leading figures espoused a Malayan nationalism. Some fudging of the citizenship issue was done to hold the coalition together": Edwin Lee, *Singapore: The Unexpected Nation* (Singapore: Institute of Southeast Asian Studies, 2008), p. 55.

30. http://www.theooifamily.com/ThePenangfileb/sep-2005/histr422.htm.
31. http://en.wikipedia.org/wiki/All-Malaya_Council_of_Joint_Action#People.27s_Constitution.
32. OHI, p. 181.
33. OHI, p. 182.
34. Malayan Security Service, Political Intelligence Journal No. 10 of 1948, 31 May 1948, CO 537/3752.
35. OHI, p. 66.
36. OHI, p. 66.
37. OHI, p. 71.
38. Ahmad Boestamam, *Carving the Path to the Summit*, translated with an introduction by William R. Roff (Athens: Ohio University Press, 1979), pp. 104–6.
39. Malayan Security Service, Political Intelligence Journal No. 12 of 1948, 30 June 1948.
40. Malayan Security Service, Political Intelligence Journal No. 13 of 1948, 15 July 1948.
41. Interview with Leon Comber at the Institute of Southeast Asian Studies.
42. OHI, p. 187.
43. https://history.state.gov/milestones/1945-1952/truman-doctrine; https://history.state.gov/departmenthistory/short-history/truman.
44. http://educ.jmu.edu/~vannorwc/assets/ghist%20102-150/pages/readings/zhdanovspeech.html.
45. Larisa Efimova, "Did the Soviet Union Instruct Southeast Asian Communists to Revolt? New Russian Evidence on the Calcutta Youth Conference of February 1948", *Journal of Southeast Asian Studies*, 40, no. 3 (2009): 468.
46. Hong Bee Lim, *Born Into War* (London: Excalibur, 1994), pp. 349–50.
47. Karl Hack, "The Origins of the Asian Cold War: Malaya 1948", *Journal of Southeast Asian Studies*, 40, no. 3 (2009): 484.
48. OHI, p. 55.
49. OHI, pp. 73–74.

50. Michael Stenson, *The 1948 Communist Revolt in Malaya: A Note on Historical Sources and Interpretation*, with a Reply by Gerald de Cruz (Singapore: Institute of Southeast Asian Studies, November 1971), p. 8.
51. Ibid., p. 12.
52. Ibid., p. 20.
53. Ibid., p. 21.
54. Ibid., p. 22.
55. Ibid., p. 23.
56. Ibid., pp. 23–24.
57. Gerald de Cruz, *Facing Facts in Malaya* (London: Union of Democratic Control, 1952), p. 4.
58. Ibid., p. 11.

Chapter 5

GOING ABROAD

De Cruz met Coral Phipps, a girl from Penang, at her cousin's house in Kuala Lumpur, fell in love with her, and asked her to marry him. She pointed out all the impossible-to-scale barriers. He did not have a job, any money in the bank, and could be picked up by the police at any time.[1] Then, Coral had promised herself that if she survived the Japanese Occupation, she would travel around the world a bit. From Penang she had moved to Kuala Lumpur and then Singapore, where de Cruz had found her a job in the Social Welfare Department. A three-year courtship followed. He asked her to marry him and they would see the world together by working their way around. He told her also that he wanted to visit the Soviet Union to find out from the horse's mouth why the MCP had taken to the jungles. She made a bargain with him. This was August 1948. By the end of that year, one or both of them should have gone abroad. If he left first, she would join him. They would get married and make their way to the Soviet Union.

De Cruz began to look for a job to finance the trip. Doors in Singapore were closed to him because of his reputation as the leader of the Eurasian Progressive Movement, the MDU and the PMCJA. But, one day, he ran into Jacob Ballas, an old friend who was now working for the Sun Life Assurance Company of Canada, which had a large branch office in Singapore. Ballas gave him a job — selling life insurance to the Malacca millionaires whom de Cruz had got to know. He took up the offer and, in Malacca, again met Tan Cheng Lock, whose friends bought two or three large policies from him. Ballas was disappointed when de Cruz told him that he was leaving Singapore, but accepted his decision. It was towards the end of 1948. He decided to go to Karachi and visit his INA friend, Inayat Hassan, who had saved him from the pursuing Japanese soldiers at Saigon. Meanwhile, Coral continued working as confidential secretary to Sir Percy McNiece, the last Governor of Singapore. She planned to save enough in six months to join de Cruz.

To cut his expenses, de Cruz took the ship to Madras (as Chennai was known then), from where he planned to take the train to Bombay (Mumbai now) and then a flight to Karachi. His good friend, the Communist P.V. Sharma, who had been holidaying in his native India, received him at Madras. So did the Indian Special Branch, which arrested both of them. Police officers, who had intimate knowledge about his activities in Malaya, grilled him on his investigation of a police shooting in a remote rubber estate in northern Johor in which eight rubber tappers had been killed. They stripped and searched him to see whether he had any Communist material or arms on him. When they found that he was in transit through India, they let him go.

Landing in Karachi on New Year's Day, 1949, he realized that he had Inayat's office address — 156 Macleod Road — but not his home address. The business district would be closed on the holiday, his taxi driver told him. Nevertheless, since that was the only address that he had, he went there. To his utter surprise and delight, Inayat's office was open and there was a party on inside. This was to toast the opening of his new firm, Advertisers & Publishers Ltd. Inayat welcomed him warmly and hired him as manager on the spot.

Coral joined him in Pakistan six months later, in June 1949, and they were married in Karachi on 2 July. Even the marriage was not free of the drama that seemed to accompany him everywhere. Stepping out on Macleod Road to buy the wedding ring, about which he had forgotten completely, he was halfway across the road when a car came hurtling towards him from a side lane without warning. He thought that that was the end. Then, just as the car was almost upon him, he slipped on a discarded banana peel on the street and fell, but managed to twist his body so that he fell lengthwise to the car. It roared over him, its high chassis passing over him with barely half an inch to spare, but the four wheels missing him completely. Helped by a passer-by, he tottered into a jewellery shop and bought the ring.

Soon, there would be more drama. Returning from a weeklong honeymoon in Hyderabad, in Sindh province, the couple found the Pakistan Special Branch waiting for them with deportation orders. The Commonwealth Office had informed it that a notorious Bolshevik and dangerous Communist agent was believed to be in Karachi. They checked it out and found it to be true. Since de Cruz and his wife were not Pakistani citizens, they were being deported. He explained to the officers that he had spent the little money that he had had on the marriage ceremony, the wedding reception and the honeymoon. He pleaded to be allowed to work in Karachi for another six months at least, but the police did not relent. Either he and his wife would leave in a few days or they would be shipped back to Singapore.

De Cruz's Karachi friends, Inayat Hassan and the rich Akbar Patel, passed the hat around and raised about a hundred pounds sterling. Patel also paid for the couple's passage by ship to Basra in Iraq, whence they would take the train to Istanbul on their way to the Soviet Union, which shared a border with Turkey. Inayat saw them off on the ship, but there was no sign of Patel. At 1:30 a.m., a very drunk Patel barged his way on to the ship and insisted that they have a last drink together ashore. The ship would leave in four hours. The couple got into Patel's car, which ran out of petrol. The petrol station was closed, but Patel managed to get hold of the owner and buy two gallons at black market prices. The driver was sacked on the spot, and Patel drove on to his house. It was 2:45 a.m. The last drink turned out to be the first of many, at the end of which their host was soundly asleep. It was 3:30 a.m., and they had just two hours to get back to the ship. They managed to wake up Patel, who promptly insisted that they all visit Inayat. On this happy occasion, the driver got his job back, they drove to Inayat's house and, having met him again, left for the ship at 4:10 a.m. There was less than an hour to go, but they sped towards the harbour through the deserted streets of Karachi. They were back on the ship on time.

The voyage to Basra was uneventful, as was the day that the couple spent in Baghdad, from which they left for Istanbul. The Baghdad Express travelled to Syria, where they spent half an hour in historical Aleppo. The border crossing into Turkey was a "belly dance" as the train crossed and re-crossed the border — eighteen times over fifteen hours in which only twenty miles were covered. It was not the railway line that had cut the Turko-Syrian border, but the border drawn up after World War I that had cut the existing railway line. Coral de Cruz suddenly realized that their passports had not been returned to them since the last stop almost two hours ago. The train conductor soon appeared, carrying a pile of passports but, horror or horrors, he lost his balance as the train swerved and lurched, and fell against an open window.

Hundreds of passports flew out. De Cruz pulled the emergency communication cord and the train came to a stop a mile away. He and the conductor went back in search of the passports, all of which they found. He was received as a hero when he returned to his carriage.

After having passed through Ankara, the Baghdad Express arrived at Haydarpaşa Station in Istanbul, three days and nights after having left Baghdad. The couple admired the architectural marvels of Istanbul before crossing the Sea of Marmara on a ferry to find their way to the border between Turkey and Soviet Armenia. The border was bristling with guns. No one was allowed to cross it without a visa, which they did not have. They returned to Istanbul.

The couple presented themselves at the Soviet Consulate-General in Istanbul in the hope of gaining a visa. The Consul-General himself received them. He told them that their application for a visa would have to be sent to Moscow. A reply would take at least a year. And that reply would certainly be a "no".

Since getting into the Soviet Union from an anti-communist country like Turkey now looked impossible, de Cruz decided to try his luck from a friendly country in Eastern Europe. He and his wife crossed the Mediterranean Sea from Istanbul to Athens to make their way to Rome and thence to Eastern Europe.

In Athens, the couple revisited the founts of Western civilization. They also encountered Western rudeness, or so it seemed, when a European trying to get to the head of a queue butted de Cruz on the shoulder. The man apologized, explaining that he was short-sighted. The de Cruzes quickly became friends with Richard Slánský and his wife, Anna. Slánský, chargé d'affaires at the Czech Embassy in Teheran, had been expelled from his post after having run up against certain Iranian officials. He and his Polish wife were returning to Prague.

De Cruz laid all his cards on the table. He told Slánský his background and that he and his wife were on their way to the Soviet Union. Could Slánský, an official from a Communist country, help them get in? Instead, Slánský, whose elder brother, Rudolf, was secretary-general of the Communist Party of Czechoslovakia, invited them to visit Czechoslovakia, where they could see the work of socialist reconstruction for themselves. The country was not yet welcoming tourists, but he could pull a few strings and get them visas and scholarships at Charles University in Prague. Then they could return to Singapore and Malaya better qualified and able to lead the Communist movement. They agreed.

They parted from their new friends in Naples after having received their address in Prague. Richard Slánský said that their visas for Czechoslovakia would be sent to the Czech Embassy in Rome.

After two days in Naples, de Cruz and his wife arrived in Rome. There, he ran into his boyhood friend, Wilbur Boswell, who had won a Queen's Scholarship to Cambridge and was now studying for the priesthood at the Jesuit College in Rome. Boswell guided them around Rome and took them on hiking trips around it.

The promised visas had arrived in Rome, and the de Cruzes were soon in Prague.

There, what awaited them was the nastiest experience in even their admittedly improbable journey to the Soviet Union. It broke de Cruz's very faith in Communism as a system of organizing human life.

When he and his wife looked up Anna Slánský, she was crying bitterly, but all that she would say was that her husband was busy. The truth was that he was under arrest, and for no other reason than that he was the brother of Rudolf Slánský, who had been overthrown in a Moscow-directed purge. In the aftermath of Yugoslav leader Josip Broz Tito's break with the Soviet

Union's domination of his country's political system, Josef Stalin decided to stop more defections in the satellite states of Central Europe. This was accomplished through a wave of purges of the national Communist leaderships that was justified by an equally convenient series of show trials. In Czechoslovakia, Rudolf Slánský had been arrested, charged with high treason, and sentenced to death. Richard Slánský had been sentenced to life imprisonment.

Richard Slánský's last act before his arrest was to have stood as guarantor for the de Cruzes. They would feel the consequences immediately. Early one morning there was a knock on the door of their hotel room. Two men from the Secret Police were standing outside. They escorted the de Cruzes to the police station, cancelled their three-month visas and gave them three days to get out of Czechoslovakia, failing which they would go to jail. The hapless couple explained that they had depended on their friend Richard Slánský and were now down and out. They had subsisted on only one meal a day, consisting of one slice of bread and a few carrots. They did not have money for even a train ticket out of Czechoslovakia. The police were unimpressed with their desperation. They would have to leave in three days, they were told. Matters would be worse if they ran away or tried to hide themselves.

Next morning, the de Cruzes thought that they had been saved when, on the front page of a Czech newspaper, they saw the face of Lim Hong Bee. He was arriving in Prague that morning to attend a meeting. They found him and explained their predicament. He was stunned but demanded to know why de Cruz had arrived in Czechoslovakia without his permission. He had had no right to leave Singapore. This was not an unreasonable position, but de Cruz still hoped that Lim would help him. After a lot of argument, Lim agreed to meet him again the following day. He did not turn up. Infuriated, de Cruz went to the police, who found Lim over the telephone. He said flatly that he could do nothing. That was the last de Cruz saw of him till they met in London a few months later.

So, the de Cruzes were being left to the tender mercies of the Czech Secret Police. Here, their story took such an unexpected turn that no one would have believed it had it appeared in a novel. But truth is indeed stranger than fiction. On the fourth morning after they had been warned to leave, de Cruz woke up at six screaming in agony. He had a terrible pain in the lumbar region on both sides of his spine. His wife summoned the manager, who called an ambulance that took them to Prague General Hospital. De Cruz was diagnosed as suffering from a stone in the kidney. The doctors kept him in hospital for seven days while they dissolved the stone.

Meanwhile, the police had turned up at his hotel at 8 a.m. on the day when he was taken to hospital. The hotel manager told them what had occurred. They arrested another foreign couple living in the hotel, an English vet married to a Pakistani doctor.

When de Cruz returned to his hotel the police were waiting for him. They gave him and his wife three more days to get out of the country. The de Cruzes called on the other couple, who had since been released but given deportation orders. Arthur and Shireen Hayward were packing — and hopping mad. They were both staunch supporters of the Communist Party of Great Britain who had been holidaying in Eastern Europe to see Communism first-hand. Everything had gone well for them till their run-in with the Czech police.

As the two couples shared their travails with each other, the Haywards helped out. They went out and sold a few souvenirs that they had bought. With that money, they bought two train tickets for de Cruz and his wife. The four of them left Prague together for England, where the Haywards hosted the de Cruzes for a week in their home in a little village called Sundon, forty miles from London. Soon, Gerald and Coral de Cruz found jobs, and their lives in Britain began.

Note

1. Material for this chapter is drawn from OHI, pp. 78–97; and *CW*, pp. 80–133.

Chapter 6

THE ENGLISH YEARS

On arrival in London, Gerald de Cruz began to look for a job. He rang up a British Army officer, a member of the Communist Party of Great Britain, who had made contact with him in Kuala Lumpur. Since he was a medical man, he asked de Cruz whether he would be interested in a job in the ancillary medical services. He got a job as an unqualified teacher in the Fountain Hospital for Mentally-Retarded Children in London. He also won a scholarship for a diploma in teaching such children.[1]

The racism that greeted his presence at a course run at the National Association for Mental Health (NAMH) headquarters was unbelievable! His English colleagues resented the fact that he could speak and write English better than they could, although he was from a "backward" colony. Matters came to a head during lectures on child psychology given by a Hilda Clarke, the senior psychologist at the association. When she offered to test the Intelligence Quotient (IQ) of any volunteer from the students, almost all his colleagues shouted out de Cruz's name. If he fared badly, their prejudice would be vindicated; if he refused to take the test, he would be branded a coward. There was a burst of ironical cheering when he accepted the challenge. During the three hours during which he underwent the comprehensive Wechsler-Bellevue Diagnostic Tests, his fellow-students copied down the questions and answers. Among those who did not share their hostility was a twenty-eight-year-old Dane, Nils Christiansen, a fellow foreigner.

The test results were released two weeks later. De Cruz did quite well in motor and manual dexterity, scoring 120, the average score being 100 and the best possible 180 and above. In memory, vocabulary, calculation, general knowledge and so on, Clarke was unable to give him a score because he scored a perfect 100 per cent, which meant that she was not able to find the limits for his intelligence! "I don't know his intellectual potential", she continued. "All I can say is that he has the intelligence to function as a Minister in our present Labour Government." The class was silent. "Not a single cheer greeted this statement from our tutor." Only Christiansen congratulated him. He thanked Heaven for his extensive reading habits and the years that he had spent rabble-rousing in Malaya and Singapore. They had stood him in good stead during the tests. When the final examinations were held at the end of the year, he passed out top of the class, with two credits — in motor and manual dexterity — and eleven distinctions. "But with my wife's cooperation, I'd already won a greater prize by far: on December 18, 1951, Coral had given birth to our first child, Judith, who was born with a full head of brown curls, and screaming her lungs out." The staid English nurses were astonished, but his wife simply told them that Judith de Cruz was just taking after her father.[2]

No less than four chapters of *Colliding Worlds* are devoted to de Cruz's work with intellectually handicapped children at Osborne House in Hastings, where he became Principal of the School Department. What shines through in the chapters is the resilience of his humanism, his stubborn faith in human nature in spite of his disenchantment with Communism, and his particular love for children sidelined by society and even their own parents. Before World War II, Conservative governments had treated hospitals like the Fountain Hospital — which had sponsored de Cruz's training — as dumping grounds for intellectually handicapped children. It was only with the return of the Labour Government after the war that Britain enunciated a new philosophy towards children, under which all of them were to be educated in a way that suited their age, aptitude and ability. It was in that happy break with history that de Cruz found his calling. He and his colleagues based their "esteem for our children not on what they could do, but rather on what they were — children first and foremost — who were dogged by handicaps of an intellectual, physical and social nature that were none of their doing".[3]

De Cruz instituted a social programme at Osborne House that included monthly football matches against teams drawn from regular schools; weekly church services on Sunday afternoon; annual holiday camps that were a fortnight long; and a special birthday celebration for every child. Birthdays were particularly important. De Cruz was troubled deeply by the fact that although most of the parents of the children had forgotten them, the children could not forget their parents. And what could be more tangible in that relationship than the birthday? De Cruz was touched when all his fifty students, except for two who were unable due to their disabilities, surprised him with the birthday song on 20 February 1952. One of them, Roy Fox, took out a battered envelope from his pocket. Inside was an old necktie — which had been a present for Roy himself a year earlier. De Cruz's "birthday programme" took off. He was helped ably in his project by a boy named Peter Davies, whose hobby was to collect birthdays! Peter could not read or write, and so committed to memory the birth dates of all his fellow students, the nurses, the teachers and the administrative staff. That meant about seventy-five people in all, quite an achievement in a boy who was said to be intellectually disabled. De Cruz got Peter to give him a week's notice of every birthday at Osborne House. Armed with permission to spend five shillings on each child, de Cruz would take the child to the Woolworths branch in Hastings for the boy to choose his present, to which the teachers would add their own presents and birthday cards. On the big day, de Cruz would make the announcement at the school assembly, the boy would face the class, and the birthday song would be sung. He would receive his presents and cards, three cheers would be raised for him, the school cook would bake a special birthday cake for him at teatime, and the song would be sung once more. "His day having passed in a daze of glory and happiness, the birthday boy would fall asleep with his birthday card clutched firmly in his hand. Usually, he was smiling when he fell asleep."[4]

That angelic vision reappeared when de Cruz decided that his students would attend church, rather than have lay preachers come and preach to them. Indeed, there would be a special children's service every week "with a minimum of sermonizing and a maximum of singing hymns and choruses".[5] A friendly vicar agreed to this, and the children began to attend church at 3 p.m. every Sunday. Since the children could not read or write, the teachers got them to memorize the hymns and choruses. The children were fitted out with new dresses fit to wear to church. The service was such a success that the vicar complimented the Osborne House boys for being better than able-bodied children because they were never bored. In fact, some of the boys were "adopted" by parish members and spent the day with them. "It was like a weekly trip to heaven", de Cruz writes.[6] Rumours began to circulate that a "saint" was devoting himself to the care of the children. Modestly, he said that he was merely trying to liberate the children.

That process spilled over from birthdays remembered to church to the football fields. Training intellectually disabled boys to kick a football is not difficult: to get them to play as a team is more difficult. But that is exactly what de Cruz did. Indeed, he went further and organized a match between his boys and a scratch team of able-bodied eleven-year-olds from a nearby school. Osborne House lost 2–1. A match with another school, with a scratch team of eleven-year-olds, saw de Cruz's side lose 30–0! He cried — but in joy, because, in those ninety minutes, his boys had played their best, never played dirty, and had never committed any fouls. They had scored a moral victory. In doing so, they had "come of age on the football field".[7]

De Cruz, too, had won a moral victory.

POLITICS

De Cruz spent six years in Britain between November 1949 and March 1956. He became associated with the Union of Democratic Control, a pressure group within the British Labour Party, and the Workers' Educational Association, another pro-Labour group. During the week, he taught at Osborne House. On weekends and during his annual leave, he travelled all over England and Wales, talking on the need for Malayan independence. Audrey Jupp, the secretary of the union, considered him one of her organization's most popular speakers. Jock and Millie Haston, who ran the association and looked upon him as their son, went even further. Jock told him that he was one of the finest orators produced by the Labour movement.[8]

De Cruz remembers vividly one particular meeting organized by the Communist Party that took place in Hyde Park. He was invited to speak on Malayan independence. When he arrived at the venue, he found to his dismay that the organizers had placed many other items on the agenda, he was only one on a long list of speakers on various subjects, and he was told sharply that he had only ten minutes. Incensed, he spoke for almost an hour. The audience cheered him, although the organizers were furious. By contrast, he found that his Tory audiences allowed him to speak freely and even cheered him. They lived up to the British idea of fair play. Generally, de Cruz observes, audiences in the south, including London and its suburbs, were phlegmatic in temper and restrained in applause, while audiences in Wales and in the north, such as in Yorkshire and Lancashire, would cheer him loudly, stamp their feet and queue up for his autograph. Indeed, de Cruz found himself intervening in British electoral politics when he campaigned for the Labour lawyer Lyn Mostyn, a friend who had been put up as a candidate for the parliamentary seat of Hornsey in 1951. De Cruz campaigned, megaphone in hand, against the Tory candidate, L.D. Gammans, once a leading rubber planter in Malaya, but the shrillness of his criticism backfired. Tory supporters who might not have turned out to vote in what was a safe Tory constituency did so because of de Cruz's attacks on imperialism and exploitation. Gammans increased his already substantial majority, and Lyn suffered a disastrous defeat. A chastened de Cruz realized that oratory without an understanding of local sentiments could be dangerous. Notwithstanding this experience, de Cruz himself was selected in 1955 to be the Labour candidate in Hastings, but that prospect was terminated by his unexpected return to Singapore to serve Chief Minister David Marshall. Had he known that Marshall would resign in a few months, de Cruz would never have left Britain.[9]

In the meantime, Abdul Razak Hussein, who would become Malaysia's second prime minister, had formed the Malayan Forum, an organization for Malayan students to discuss political issues, at Malaya Hall in London. De Cruz joined the forum, both listening to and giving talks on the situation in Malaya. He recalls a big clash that he had there with John Eber. Eber, who had arrived in London after having been jailed in Singapore, was at first quite amiable towards him. But when Eber found that he had left the party, he became his enemy.

Eber, Lim Hong Bee and a group of twenty like-minded people took control of the forum's organ, *Suara Merdeka*. The Communists' role in the forum was to denounce the situation in Malaya and Singapore; to fight for a united Malaya, including Singapore; and to oppose both the Alliance Government in the Federation and the Labour Front in Singapore. Hence, *Suara Merdeka*'s editorials adopted a strident position on Tunku Abdul Rahman and Malayan independence. When Goh Keng Swee, to whom de Cruz was close, arrived in London as a doctoral student, he decided that the paper's editorial board should be replaced. He collected enough signatures to call, under the forum's constitution, for an emergency meeting to pass a motion of no confidence in the board. Even though this move was backed by 177 students, twenty-three Communists almost foiled the attempt. The hall where the meeting was held had about forty chairs. The Communists, who had arrived long before the starting time of 4 p.m., occupied the chairs, leaving only seventeen chairs for the 177 students likely to oppose them. Then, they placed the vote of no confidence last on an agenda of five items, hoping to filibuster their way through the meeting and wear out their opponents. The tactic all but worked: de Cruz's group began to thin. By 7 p.m., only seventy-seven of them remained in the room. But that number was large enough to throw out the committee.

At the meeting, Eber targeted de Cruz and attacked a sentence in an article that he had written for *Suara Merdeka* a couple of weeks previously. The sentence was: "The rule of law, for which Britain has been justly famed, has always been known in Malaya, as the law of rule." But Eber quoted it as saying, "The rule of law, for which Britain has been justly famed, has always been known in Malaya." Of course, de Cruz pointed out to him that he had not concluded the sentence there, but after "Malaya", had put a comma and added the words "as the law of rule" — which changed the complexion of the sentence entirely. But Eber refused to accept that he had distorted de Cruz's meaning, claiming that all that he had done was to have changed a tiny little comma into a tiny little full-stop! De Cruz found this to be a typical Communist tactic of distortion.

Goh Keng Swee was extremely generous to de Cruz personally. He said to him, "Gerry, what are you wasting your time teaching mentally-retarded children for? I've got a proposition for you. You must join the PAP. In the next elections we're going to sweep the board and we're going to take the government of Singapore over, and we want you in with us. Now, I'm here on a Fellowship to do my Doctorate, but I am also getting my pay as a civil servant. So I will finance you to take up Law studies. You can complete them in two years or two-and-a-half years, and then you can go back to Malaya and we can all be together in the PAP and work for our country."[10] But de Cruz turned down the offer, saying that he had a wife and a child to think of and it would not be fair on Goh to support all of them. But the real reason was that de Cruz had burned his fingers with Communism and was not confident of his political judgement anymore. He did not wish to be involved directly with any political party in Singapore.

De Cruz also met Toh Chin Chye, another member of the Malayan Forum. Toh struck him as a very sincere and enthusiastic person who was learning his politics in London. On one occasion, the forum invited Lee Kuan Yew, who had just graduated with his wife from Cambridge, to speak. Lee gave a brilliant speech, but de Cruz did not meet him personally, although he knew Lee's wife, who had studied for the Queen's Scholarship with him for three years at Raffles Institution. De Cruz also met T.T. Rajah, who kept company with titled people in the Conservative Party, wore a bowler hat and carried a rolled black umbrella. He and friends teased Rajah by saying that he mixed only with Duchesses.

While in Britain, de Cruz received a visit from Abdullah Samsudin, whose elder brother had been a fellow political-traveller with de Cruz in Malaya in the late 1940s. Abdullah, who had first met de Cruz in Penang in 1947, joined the army in 1952 and left for training in Britain the following year. He located de Cruz through Eber. Rationing of essential items such as meat and sugar was on. Since Abdullah did not cook, he handed his ration cards along with some cash to Coral when he visited the de Cruz family on weekends. "Coral was a fine cook", he recalls in an interview from Kuala Lumpur, where he is now based.[11] "Her beef curry and beef sausages with potatoes were all that I needed to eat with bread and rice." He also followed de Cruz on his lecture trail for the Labour Party. Many years later, Abdullah, who rose to be a Lieutenant-General, helped to bring together de Cruz and Sarawak Chief Minister Abdul Rahman Ya'kub, who invited de Cruz to work for the Sarawak Foundation in Kuching.

In 1955 de Cruz wrote to David Marshall, whose younger brothers had been his childhood friends. Marshall, whom de Cruz had approached to ask him to join the MDU in 1946, had declined because the war was over, he had to start his legal career anew, and he had no time for politics. So de Cruz was surprised when Marshall had come into politics after all, and from the top, starting off as Chief Minister. De Cruz wrote to him to say that he was in London, and that he would be glad to do anything he could for Marshall in his capacity as Chief Minister. He received a very urgent telegram from him, saying: "COME BACK TO SINGAPORE IMMEDIATELY AND HELP ME. I AM SURROUNDED BY CROOKS AND I NEED AN HONEST MAN BY MY SIDE." Knowing Marshall, de Cruz decided to put the screws on. He sent him a telegram saying (this was not true): "HAVE RESIGNED MY JOB. PLEASE SEND AIR FARE." He got a screaming telegram saying: "PLEASE HOLD YOUR HORSES. I HAVEN'T YET CONSULTED THE LABOUR FRONT CENTRAL COMMITTEE ABOUT EMPLOYING YOU, AND I HAVE TO GET THEIR CONSENT BEFORE I DO SO."

But Marshall really wanted de Cruz to come. He wrote to him in June 1955:

> You can help. You can come out here as organizing secretary of the Labour Front and the TUC [Trades Union Congress]. It may well be that once here your somewhat impatient nature would prefer the PAP. I do not know, but I do think that your place is here to take a hand in guiding the future. I have known you to be corroded with bitterness to the point where you were no longer useful as a human being. The tone of your letter does indicate that your soul is now healed, and that you have attained maturity. If that is true, you can be a very very real help. If you are interested I would indicate that the present Labour Front is an extremely tenuous organization and it has no money in its coffers. I will be personally responsible for such expenses as may be incurred for the first year, including your salary.[12]

The Labour Front's executive rejected Marshall's proposal in July 1955 and British Intelligence in Singapore, too, advised him against employing de Cruz, saying that he was a Communist and could not be trusted. Marshall asked Hilda Selwyn-Clarke to meet de Cruz to find out whether he had really changed. She found him evasive about his past.[13] So Marshall wrote to him, saying: "This is the opinion about you. Would you please give me your solemn oath that you are not a Communist?" De Cruz wrote back: "Yes, I do. But what's the use of it? If I am a Communist, I'll swear anything as long as I could get back to Singapore to be in a close position in the Labour Front in order to destroy it from within. So it doesn't make any difference whether I give you this assurance or I don't."[14]

De Cruz met Marshall and Lim Yew Hock when they arrived in London for negotiations with the British. Lim was an old friend whom de Cruz had known since the time he had been secretary of a clerical union in Singapore. Lim, too, advised him to return to Singapore.

That took a year. In the meanwhile, Marshall arranged for de Cruz to receive six weeks of training in party organization at the Fabian Colonial Bureau at his personal expense.[15] De Cruz knew a journalist called Andrew Roth, who had visited Singapore after the war and had gone on to establish himself in London. When he found out about de Cruz's impending return, he wrote a very laudatory article on him, giving details of what he had done in London. So when de Cruz did return to Singapore in March 1956, he received a warm reception at the airport.

Notes

1. Material for this chapter is drawn from OHI, pp. 134–38 and pp. 190–98; and *CW*, pp. 134–67.
2. *CW*, pp. 138–39.
3. *CW*, pp. 143–44.
4. *CW*, p. 150.

5. *CW*, p. 152.
6. *CW*, p. 154.
7. *CW*, p. 160.
8. *CW*, p. 161.
9. *CW*, pp. 162–67.
10. OHI, p. 196.
11. Interview, 19 April 2012.
12. David Marshall to Gerald de Cruz, 14 June 1955, cited in Kevin Y.L. Tan, *Marshall of Singapore: A Biography* (Singapore: Institute of Southeast Asian Studies, 2008), p. 291.
13. Ibid., pp. 291–92. Lady Selwyn-Clarke was the secretary of the Fabian Colonial Bureau.
14. OHI, pp. 198–99.
15. Tan, *Marshall of Singapore*, op. cit., p. 292.

Chapter 7

RETURN TO SINGAPORE

"In April 1955, David Saul Marshall, a Sephardi Jew, came into Singapore politics like a shooting star and, as in the nature of a shooting star, filled the sky with brilliance and disappeared", Chan Heng Chee writes in her biography of Singapore's first elected Chief Minister. Although Marshall was not to preside over Singapore's transition to independence, he became a popular hero, respected for his integrity, his sympathy for the underdog, and his "abiding commitment to a democratic civic culture".[1] Gerald de Cruz's work with Marshall forms an essential part of his political contribution to Singapore.

On his return to Singapore, de Cruz became the Labour Front's Organizing Secretary and Secretary of its Central Committee.[2] He was given an office in which there were thousands of applications to join the Front. They went three-quarters of the way up to the ceiling of the little room. He was asked to check them, which he duly did by rushing around Singapore trying to locate the applicants. He soon discovered that the applications were fake, with fake names, fake addresses and fake identity card numbers. They had apparently been faked by the Lim Yew Hock group to make him President of the Front. Then, he met people like Mak

Pak Shee who had strong secret society connections and were open about them. Mak said to him that he had been supported all his life by secret societies. So now that he was a junior minister, the least he could do was to pay them back for all that they had done for him.

All this occurred against the wider backdrop of David Marshall's fight for complete independence for Singapore. He explained to de Cruz later that partial independence would not resolve Singapore's problems because its strong Communist underground movement and the pro-Communists leading the radical Chinese middle-school students would portray partial independence as no independence. Only real independence could placate "the anti-imperialist sentiments of the pro-Communists". Although half a loaf is better than no bread, Marshall felt that, in the volatile situation that Singapore was in, "the bread we needed was independence, and half a loaf of independence would be no loaf at all".[3]

Marshall went to London for talks with the Colonial Secretary. Everywhere he travelled, he made a speech threatening to resign if Singapore did not get independence. The Central Committee of the Labour Front was worried because he had not consulted it on his threatened resignation (although he might have brought up the issue of independence) and he would have to keep his word if he failed. Indeed, that is what occurred: He was asked to resign when he was unsuccessful. Marshall did so very reluctantly because his tactic had only been a ploy. In the event, though, the committee voted unanimously that he should resign, and Lim Yew Hock took his place.

Marshall was dead set against the negotiations that Lim Yew Hock and Lee Kuan Yew held in London in 1957, because the negotiations were not over full independence, and he resigned from the Labour Front because he could not agree with what had been obtained. Marshall challenged Lee in the Legislative

Assembly because "he wanted to show that the people of Singapore supported him in the demand for complete independence" and because apparently — so de Cruz had been informed at that time — "the Communists said they would support him if he opposed Lee Kuan Yew. But then at the last moment they withdrew their pledge to support him. And he withdrew from his challenge because he felt that without Communist support, he couldn't beat Lee Kuan Yew."[4]

Having resigned from the Labour Front, Marshall set up the Workers' Party. Why did de Cruz not join it?

> Well, you see, when I came back, I came back solely to support a friend — David Marshall. And I didn't see myself as joining any particular political party, but just helping David Marshall in his campaign. Once he resigned from the Labour Front and left me to handle the crooks that he'd left behind him in the Labour Front, I wasn't keen on joining him on any of his further adventures. I felt it was a great shame that he had put himself into this position, where he was forced to resign from the Labour Front.... Well, I thought it was very stupid of David to go off on his own and demand total independence, threaten to resign, and then he resigned. He went away for three months to China. He came back and began to form his Workers' Party. I suppose you can say I lost confidence in him. It never occurred to me to join the Workers' Party.[5]

De Cruz gave an example of how Marshall led the party. He used to have an open house for his friends at his home in Changi every Sunday. One Sunday, a van full of the other members of the party's Central Committee came in to consult him over an urgent issue. Marshall was very annoyed that they had come to his house on a Sunday when he was entertaining his friends and asked them to meet him the following day. "I think the great pity about David Marshall is that he came into politics from the top. He began as Chief Minister and then in his response to events, gradually worked himself down. Whereas if he had worked himself up from the bottom, he would have probably made a far better politician."[6]

Intriguingly, Marshall believed that de Cruz had been the main instigator behind his departure from office. During the Chinese Middle schools disturbances, when there was a curfew, de Cruz spent the three days and three nights at Marshall's flat. One day, Marshall cornered him in his bedroom. "Gerry", he said, "you were the person who pulled me down from the post of Chief Minister, weren't you?" De Cruz replied: "No, David. There was such a person. But it wasn't me." Curious, Marshall asked: "Who was it? Who was it?" De Cruz replied: "It was yourself. You kept threatening that you would resign if you failed. And you did fail. And we just thought that you should keep to your word."[7] It "was a matter in which all the Central Committee members concurred without the question of me persuading them to do so. Francis Thomas, Lim Yew Hock, [Armand Joseph] Braga, Chew Swee Kee — they all felt the same way." However, it was a "bitter mistake" because "once we lost David, we lost the major element, certainly in the public eye, of integrity and honesty. And yet it was because of those very circumstances, because he was such an honest man, because he was a man of such integrity that we thought he ought to resign to keep to that reputation. But we never saw what a terrible impact it would have on the Labour Front; what a severe blow it would be to public confidence in the Labour Front."[8] But Marshall's suspicions lingered. De Cruz, whose wife was Marshall's confidential secretary, used to accompany her to his home on Sundays. Marshall told her one day that he could not have de Cruz over any more. She replied that, in that case, she would not come either. So the couple stopped going to Marshall's house for several months, till "one Christmas (Oh David!) he came rushing around looking for us in order to invite us back to his parties once more — Sunday open house. And then we resumed going to his home on Sundays." Although Marshall believed that "I was the key mover in what he called the conspiracy to force him to resign as Chief Minister of the Labour Front", now "we are very good friends again".[9]

Throughout his Oral History Interview, de Cruz spoke movingly about Marshall.

> David Marshall was not a politician as it were by vocation. He was swept into politics as the clamour for independence arose, and he was a very astute and imaginative man who was always about 10 steps ahead of the rest of his Central Committee. So he would take decisions which afterwards the Central Committee had to rectify, instead of it being the other way round, you see. So he was very much a one-man band so to speak. He was the conductor, he was the composer, he was the first violinist, he was the orchestra, and the rest were there to applaud or not to applaud. Extremely honest, passionately honest, with a tremendous flair for public relations.[10]

But Marshall could also go overboard. On his trip to China in 1956 after stepping down as Chief Minister, he had an argument with Premier Zhou Enlai. Marshall shouted at Zhou, who smiled at him. Then Marshall banged the table; Zhou kept smiling. "So there you are, you see. David Marshall was merely the Chief Minister, the ex–Chief Minister to boot of a tiny pimple on the surface of Asia known as Singapore. And he was confronting the Prime Minister of the greatest, most populous nation on earth. And he had the impertinence to lose his temper with him and to bang the table when he was a guest in that country. Well, that was David. He wore his heart on a sleeve. And he was a most lovable man."[11]

There was a marked difference between Marshall's and Lim's leadership styles:

> The difference between David Marshall and Lim Yew Hock first lay in the fact that David Marshall was a kind of inspired amateur at politics. But because of his professional renown as a lawyer, because of his transparent honesty, because of his great flair for oratory, and above all, his flair for public relations, the people of Singapore believed in him, and as long as David Marshall was the Chief Minister and the leader of the Labour Front, the Labour Front had some prestige and had some standing. Without David Marshall, once he resigned and Lim Yew Hock took over, then the rot began to set in. Because Lim Yew Hock was a very intelligent man, and in himself a very nice man, but he didn't have the reputation for honesty and intelligence and integrity that David Marshall had. Also, Lim Yew Hock mixed up [*sic*] with people like Mak Pak Shee and Lee Yew Seng and company, that had very bad reputation[s] because of their secret society connections, and this rubbed off on him considerably.[12]

It affected Lim's relations with others as well. Singapore Trades Union Congress (STUC) president S. Jaganathan and other moderate trade union leaders had tremendous admiration and respect for Marshall, but were unhappy over Lim's links with Mak Pak Shee and Lee Yew Seng.

De Cruz recalled an incident that dramatized the difference between Marshall and Lim. Under the Rendell Constitution, there was no official post of Chief Minister; there were various ministers under the Governor, who had the final say and could veto everything. But for convenience sake, in order to talk to the Governor, the Minister for Commerce was also called the Chief Minister. When Marshall became the Minister for

Commerce because the Labour Front had won the elections, he was automatically given the title "Chief Minister", too. He had a nice office as Minister for Commerce but none as Chief Minister. He went to the Governor to ask for one, and was told to be satisfied with what he had. So what Marshall did was to take a table and a chair and put them under the stairs of the Legislative Assembly building. In an instant, he had captured the imagination and the sympathy of the people of Singapore. He spent a few days under the stairs and when the Governor still refused to budge, he threatened to take the table, the chair and his office boy and set up office in the midst of the Padang, running Singapore from there! The Governor caved in. George Thomson, Director of Public Relations, was bundled out of his office, and Marshall moved in. Marshall had got his way.

Lim Yew Hock's style was different. One Saturday, de Cruz received word that the Chief Minister wanted to see him urgently. He arrived in Lim's office at five minutes past one. The staff had gone home. He knocked at the office door, and went in.

> Now, what did I see? In the centre of the Chief Minister's office, there was a large conference table. On that conference table a man was lying fast asleep. He had his coat off and he was in a sleeveless singlet. And he had his shoes and socks off, and he had his trousers rolled up like this, and he was lying fast asleep in the centre of the conference table — looking for all the world like somebody in a Chinese coffee-shop, a coffee-shop man.
>
> But as I turned round to Saman (the office boy) to ask him what was happening, I thought to myself, "That fellow seems familiar." So I walked up to him, and it was the Chief Minister of Singapore, Lim Yew Hock, lying and snoring slightly in the centre of that table.
>
> So I woke him up and I said, "Lim Yew Hock, what is it you wanted to see me about?"

> And he opened his eyes sleepily, "Oh Gerry, it's you."
>
> Then lying down there, he began talking to me for a few minutes. Told me what he wanted from me. I've forgotten what it is. And then I said goodbye and he went back to his sleep and I went out of the office."[13]

De Cruz added that Lim Yew Hock's courage in jailing pro-Communist leaders in the PAP "allowed Lee Kuan Yew a new lease of life and thus saved Singapore for Lee Kuan Yew and the PAP".[14] But why would Lim help the PAP? De Cruz speculated that he was probably advised by the Special Branch to do this, particularly by Richard Corridon, an Englishman who had tremendous admiration for the political genius of Lee Kuan Yew.

> It is possible (I'm only saying it) that Richard Corridon was the man who advised Lim Yew Hock that for the sake of Singapore, we should get rid of the Communists. And maybe, nobody perhaps realised that out of this situation, Lee Kuan Yew would re-build the PAP to such an extent. I don't know what the calculations were and who were the advisers. I was not one of them certainly. It was done very quietly. I mean, the decision to do such a thing, of course, was not communicated to us. It was very top ministerial level. And probably only in the first place, the decision taken by Lim Yew Hock with people like Corridon advising him. I'm not sure about it."[15]

As for relations between David Marshall and Lee Kuan Yew, they "were at loggerheads always — they were like oil and water; neither could really understand the other". Marshall felt that Lee was "playing games" with the Communists, who would eventually swallow up Lee and his group. However, Marshall did not believe that Lee or Goh Keng Swee or Toh Chin Chye would toe the Communist line, although they might be deceived by the Communists.[16] De Cruz, with his insider's experience of Communism, was extremely critical of the PAP's connection with the Civil Rights Convention, which had been formed before the October 1956 student riots in Chinese schools. Communist strategy was to have an underground movement which functioned in secret, but also above-ground front organizations with a democratic appearance. One of their favourite ploys was to start civil rights organizations to fight for the very rights which they would snuff out if they came into power. He was worried that the PAP was being taken in by the ploy. On hindsight, however, he believed that the non-Communist PAP leaders had gone along with the convention to play the Communist game.

But why did de Cruz not join the PAP? It was because the party was working with the Communists. He did not believe that Lee Kuan Yew was himself a Communist.

> But from all my previous experience, I had come to believe that those who worked with Communists were eventually swallowed up by the Communists and that this was inevitable. Because the Communists are much more disciplined, because they have a political strategy, because they are much more ruthless.... In 99 cases out of a hundred, the non-Communists working with the Communists in a united front so to speak, are usually swallowed up and defeated by the Communists who take over complete control. Because to the Communists the united front with non-Communists is one of their basic tactics. It's a tactic they use in order to get more mass support than they can command merely as a Communist Party. And to them it's merely tactical, merely a step towards complete Communist control. Because they are more disciplined, because they are more ruthless, because they are more organised, when they eventually come into conflict with the non-Communists, most of the time they win.[17]

De Cruz recalled receiving a call one morning in 1958 from Lee Kuan Yew, who wanted to meet him at about eleven at night at the eighth milestone on Upper Thomson Road. Lee arrived, invited him into his car and drove off to MacRitchie Reservoir. The reason for the location: Lee did not want the Communists to know that he was meeting de Cruz. Lee said: "I want to talk to you about David Marshall. I can't understand him. To me, he must be a mad man. But I understand that you've known him all your life. So can you please tell me what makes David Marshall tick?" De Cruz told him what he thought about Marshall. He added that if Lee would stop flirting with the Communists, "things could be very much better between him and the rest of us". Lee replied that everybody would understand once he put all his cards on the table. De Cruz advised him not to delay too long because people then might mistrust him whatever cards he showed. They drove back, Lee dropped him off at his car, and de Cruz drove off.[18]

Mrs Jean Marshall was a "dear and deep friend" of Coral de Cruz, whom she describes as a "very ethical, lovely, caring, positive, intelligent woman who, if her education had not been chewed up by the War, would have been at least as high an achiever academically and otherwise, as her two noteworthy children". She speaks of a complex relationship between their husbands.

> Gerry and David both resisted colonialism and colonial attitudes. David did not see the future in extreme Left terms and was never lured by the extreme Left. I think it was probably his ethical Jewish and in some ways British-style ideas that made him throughout his post-WW2 life value above all basic democracy, and stand for the worth and validity of the individual. Gerry was someone who thought in terms of systems, which David in some ways didn't. Gerry was an extraordinary man — whatever

> he believed he believed with complete and absolute conviction. The fact that a few years previously he had believed something completely different never bothered him at all. But he was not a conscious chameleon. He had just changed his convictions. This was not what we often call two-facedness. But David, who had also known him pre-Occupation, did not have this view. He found these changes absolutely infuriating. They were both men with a lot of emotional component. Gerry's changeableness in conviction was not something David could feel positive about.
>
> Gerry was a very complicated person, a man of inconsistent enthusiasms at times. But his contradictions never seemed to me to have been dishonest. Some people were indeed unable to see the sincerity of the chameleon as I did and saw it as expedient dishonesty. I liked him. He was an exciting and engaging person even when frustratingly contradictory; but there was always an absolute conviction behind what he was doing. It was real to him.

Mrs Marshall adds that she is speaking of the period from 1956 to 1965; she had far less contact with de Cruz after Coral's untimely death.[19]

Soon after Marshall's departure from political office, de Cruz was driving with his wife and gave a lift to Norcutt Jansen, a Ceylonese living across the road from them. It was habitual for de Cruz to give people, including Jansen, lifts on his way to town because he felt guilty driving a car that was half-empty. This time, Jansen asked him whether they could speak after de Cruz's wife, now confidential secretary to Marshall, had got off at Cavenagh Bridge. Jansen asked whether de Cruz could put him in touch with Education Minister Chew Swee Kee who, he said, was avoiding him and would not make an appointment to see him. Jansen said that Chew owed him $14,000, which was a part of his commission for having helped arrange the sale of tin mines in Ipoh costing $350,000 to Chew. De Cruz went to Francis Thomas, the minister who was "the only honest man as far as I knew in the Labour Front under Lim Yew Hock".[20] Thomas was shocked and approached Lim, who said that all that he had received was $15,000, the rest being with Chew. Chew kept silent. Thomas, who could not stand it anymore, blurted out the affair to Lee Kuan Yew in a private conversation one day. Lee promptly demanded a parliamentary inquiry, at which Thomas and de Cruz were the star witnesses. Kenneth Byrne had meanwhile found out something on the issue after having made quiet investigations in the Income Tax Department. All in all, what transpired was that Chew had gone to Taiwan, where he had been paid about $750,000 by certain Taiwanese and American interests, which were planning to move into Singapore for the next elections.[21]

This was a time when politics was still new in Singapore. Many people did not understand the party system. In fact, a professor at the University of Singapore actually asked de Cruz whether Lee Kuan Yew was the leader of the Labour Front! The party had branches in various parts of Singapore. Its legislators were supposed to nurture their constituencies and hold weekly meetings, but Francis Thomas was the only person who did so seriously. The leaders of the Front were all ministers, and there was no second-level of cadres to take their place. At headquarters, de Cruz was the only full-time member of the staff, helped by a clerical assistant and an office boy. When the Front and the PAP arrived at an alliance for the City Council elections of December 1957, he gave away to Toh Chin Chye, who was representing the PAP in the negotiations over the allocation of constituencies, more seats than he had expected. This was because de Cruz believed it wrong for the Front to fight in constituencies to which it had not paid attention. This was "one of the reasons why the PAP gained such a great victory".[22] The PAP won 13 seats, the Liberal Socialist Party 7, the Labour Front 4, the Workers' Party 4, the United Malays National Organization 2, and Independents 2. The Labour Front's funds were non-existent, and so individual candidates financed their own contests. S.H. Tan, a famous eye doctor in Balestier Road, urged de Cruz to stand and promised to finance him fully. But he was not interested in direct political participation any more. With Marshall's departure, the Labour Front was sagging and was not a vital organization. It accepted the election results gracefully. Also, the poor state of party finances was one reason for Chew going to Taiwan to raise money, but when he got so much of it, he "decided to feather his own nest instead".[23]

Ong Eng Guan became Mayor after the elections. He "made a tremendous sensation" by using populist tactics, giving his supporters hawkers' licences and taxi-drivers' licences.

> And we didn't like it at all.... We didn't like his dictatorial method. And we were afraid that he might prove too strong for Lee Kuan Yew because of [the] tremendous support that he garnered as Mayor by these tactics. But there's no doubt that he'd laid the base for greater PAP support. And a lot of the credit of the PAP victory in '59 must go to Ong Eng Guan. He was a kind of a "lesser" David Marshall in a sense. He didn't have David Marshall's integrity but he had the common touch. He knew what people wanted. He played on those needs and fears and aspirations. But whereas you could tell that David Marshall was a man of integrity and honesty, one didn't feel the same way about Ong Eng Guan at all. More of a demagogue — that's the word I wanted to use.[24]

Ong Eng Guan's "sudden soaring to prominence and popularity provided a very real threat to Lee Kuan Yew. And it developed into a long drawn-out struggle between the two of them for leadership of the PAP which Lee Kuan Yew eventually won."[25]

These developments set the stage for Lim Yew Hock's formation of the Singapore People's Alliance, a coalition of the Labour Front and the Liberal Socialist Party, in November 1958. Soon after the Chew Swee Kee enquiry, Francis Thomas came to de Cruz and said: "Lim Yew Hock has asked me to close down the Labour Front so that we can all move into the [Singapore People's] Alliance. And I have written this letter to be given out as a press statement, closing down the Labour Front." De Cruz responded: "That's nonsense. Don't you realise, Francis, that if we closed down the Labour Front, then that money, which is supposed to be meant for the Labour Front, will just be swallowed up into their own pockets." Thomas did not want to touch the "contaminated money". De Cruz agreed that it was contaminated but argued that it was still meant for the party, not for individuals. He tore up the draft press statement and threw it into the wastepaper basket. So the Labour Front continued to exist, although only skeletally. Chew later wrote to Thomas offering to divide up the $750,000, with $375,000 going to the party and Chew keeping the rest. Thomas rejected the offer. So the Labour Front continued to exist until Lim Yew Hock and others formed the Singapore Alliance without resigning from the Front. "All these people were exploiting the party for personal reasons and not for the welfare of the people of Singapore." Asked why Lim Yew Hock had decided to join up with the Liberal Socialists in the Singapore People's Alliance, de Cruz replied that the Labour Front "quite clearly was totally discredited", and Lim had to seek allies wherever he could find them. "And since there was no question of political principle involved, but since they were forming another party which might possibly gain popular support, he looked around for wherever he could gain some support".[26]

In the meantime de Cruz had tried but failed to invigorate the Labour Front's branches. So he thought that if compulsory voting were introduced, then the people would be forced to learn at least a little about the party set-up. Members attending the first delegates' meeting for which de Cruz was responsible, in December 1956, supported his idea unanimously. He went to David Marshall with the resolution calling for compulsory voting. But Marshall opposed the idea because it would not be democratic. De Cruz argued that Marshall was correct in theory, but that in practice, in a new country like Singapore, what might happen was that the political system could result in a party being voted into power on a minority vote and therefore without the legitimacy, prestige and status that it would enjoy with the majority vote. But Marshall was adamant.

There was another delegates' meeting in 1957 and once more de Cruz put up the issue of compulsory voting. Once more it was unanimously supported by the branches and by all the delegates. By now, Lim was in power. But he, too, was against compulsory voting. He turned down the idea in 1958 as well. But as the elections approached in 1959, he was very worried about the rise of the PAP and instituted compulsory voting, believing that older voters, who tended to be conservative, would vote for the Labour Front. In the event, it did not work that way, and the PAP received a decisive majority. De Cruz's successful fight for compulsory voting remains one of his key contributions to politics in Singapore.

MERGER

In 1961 Tunku Abdul Rahman came to Singapore and proposed Merger with Malaysia. De Cruz was very happy because he had believed all his life that Singapore was a part of Malaya and that they should be one country. Indeed, this historic development had been preceded in his work with the Pan-Malayan Council of Joint Action, when he and his colleagues had drawn up the People's Constitution of Malaysia uniting Singapore with Malaya "in every possible sense".[27] He met Lee Kuan Yew, who asked him about his formulation of the idea of Merger, which was that "the pace of development of Malaysia must be the pace of development of the Malay peasant". De Cruz agreed with this formulation wholeheartedly. He "thought that was the right policy to follow, and that we couldn't go too fast because if the non-Malays went ahead under Malaysia and the Malays were left backward and far behind, then exclusions must necessarily occur".[28] De Cruz recalled a personal incident in this connection. In 1956 he had typed out ten things that he believed to be true about Malays. He went to the University of Singapore and met Zainal Abidin, head of the Department of Malay Studies. De Cruz asked him if his observations were correct. The answer was that half were untrue and the other half, half-true. "So there was I, totally ignorant of what makes the Malay tick."[29]

The following year, de Cruz was interviewed by an American journalist named Shirle Gordon, who had been working on the Middle East in Egypt but had her research in Cairo interrupted when Nasser came to power. De Cruz invited her to write on Islam in Malaysia. She demurred, because she was a visiting American. What deserved to be researched was how Islam affected Malays economically, educationally, culturally and socially, and the only people who could provide an answer were Malays themselves. So de Cruz initiated a project on the impact of Islam on Malays in Malaya and Singapore. He leaned on Lim Yew Hock, who in turn leaned on the Asia Foundation and the Lee Foundation, and they raised about $18,000. Gordon began work on the project with a team of Malay intellectuals, who included Zainal Abidin,

State Attorney-General Ahmad Ibrahim and Naguib Alatas. This was an early indication of de Cruz's concerns, not over Merger — which he supported wholeheartedly — but over how it would be carried out. "Later, of course, when things became difficult between UMNO and the PAP, and there were two racial riots in Singapore, I was very, very concerned because I felt we had been pushing the Malays too fast."[30] In the run-up to Merger, "many people were very doubtful". In Chinatown, "they weren't very happy about merging with Malaysia, and they felt that this would be a hindrance to Singapore. And I suppose that was proved to be true because when we were separated from Malaysia, there were reports that crackers had been fired in Chinatown to celebrate our separation from Malaysia."[31]

Notes

1. Chan Heng Chee, *A Sensation of Independence: David Marshall — A Political Biography* (Singapore and Kuala Lumpur: Times Books International, 2001), p. 1.
2. Most of the material for this chapter is drawn from OHI, pp. 102–26 and pp. 200–63.
3. OHI, p. 223. De Cruz believed that the Labour Front was in a no-win situation over the student riots. On the one hand, it had to act against Communists who were using students on the frontlines; on the other, decisive police action that led to the students getting hurt would turn the tide of public sympathy in the rioters' favour. But Lim Yew Hock had no option but to react because, otherwise, he would have been overwhelmed: OHI, pp. 226–27.
4. OHI, p. 230.
5. OHI, pp. 232–33.
6. OHI, p. 114.
7. OHI, pp. 113–14.
8. OHI, p. 114.
9. OHI, p. 260.

10. OHI, pp. 204–5.
11. OHI, p. 115.
12. OHI, p. 211.
13. OHI, p. 213.
14. OHI, pp. 213–14.
15. OHI, p. 118.
16. OHI, p. 215.
17. OHI, pp. 111–12.
18. OHI, pp. 215–17.
19. Interview with Jean Marshall, 3 December 2012.
20. OHI, p. 202.
21. See Joey Long, "The Chew Swee Kee Affair Revisited: Querying the American Involvement in Singapore", *South East Asia Research* 10, no. 2 (2002): 217–39.
22. OHI, p. 208.
23. OHI, p. 209.
24. OHI, pp. 239–40.
25. OHI, p. 241.
26. OHI, pp. 241–43.
27. OHI, p. 252.
28. OHI, p. 253.
29. OHI, p. 254.
30. OHI, p. 255.
31. OHI, p. 263.

Chapter 8

THE POLITICAL THINKER

POLITICAL STUDY CENTRE

Lee Kuan Yew recalls in his memoirs that, even before the People's Action Party took office in 1959, Goh Keng Swee, Kenny Byrne and he had decided to set up a political study centre "to teach top-ranking civil servants about the communist threat and our social and economic problems. To be successful, however, we had to win their confidence and convince them they were not simply being brainwashed".[1]

Former History lecturer George Thomson was chosen to run the centre. He was an effective teacher "because he was full of enthusiasm for whatever he taught. He understood what we wanted and soon grasped the part he had to play."[2] Thomson chose de Cruz as his assistant. Lee opened the centre, situated in a colonial government bungalow in Goodwood Hill, on 15 August 1959. Its objectives, he told civil servants, were not only to "stimulate your minds but also to inform you of the acute problems that confront any popularly elected government in a revolutionary situation.... Once these problems have been posed to you, you will be better able to help us work out the solutions to them, by making the administration more sensitive and responsive to the needs and mood of the people."[3] In a message published in the first edition of *Bakti*, the centre's journal, Goh elaborated on this point. "The Civil Servant participates in the democratic state by contributing his skill and experience in running the administrative machinery. He can hardly hope to be an effective administrator if he is unaware of the political milieu in which he must operate or if he is unsympathetic to the long-term objectives which the government sets out to achieve."[4] Lee and some of his ministers visited the centre themselves, discussing situations that had to be dealt with immediately.

In his Oral History Interview, de Cruz speaks of Thomson as "a marvellous Scotsman who came out here with Mountbatten's forces, became our first Director of Public Relations, identified himself with the aspirations of the new Singapore and became trusted by every Singapore government — the British Government, [the] David Marshall Government and [the] Lee Kuan Yew Government. He saw the centre's role as lying in understanding the changes that had taken place in Singapore. This was necessary because "the senior civil servants in particular had been brought in by the British in a Singapore in which there was no politics, in which in fact politics was regarded as a dirty word and an anti-British activity, and who naturally had developed in themselves a great fear of political understanding and knowledge". Yet, "if they were to behave neutrally, or impartially as civil servants, then they had to have some understanding of politics. Otherwise how could they in truth steer an impartial path between left and right, between different political parties and so on and so forth?" In order to understand change, they had to comprehend concepts such as imperialism, capitalism and socialism.[5]

Thomson drew up between himself and de Cruz a series of lectures and workshops to cover a two-week course. They decided to start at the top and work their way down. They began with Division One bureaucrats. It was not smooth sailing at first.

> I must confess that the very top civil servants were very snobbish. They felt it a bit demeaning to come to a course like this. If they'd been sent to England or America, of course they would have welcomed it. But to think that our own Singapore people had anything to teach them — they found that extremely difficult to swallow, except for one or two among them, like Ahmad Ibrahim.... But with several of the others, there was this sense of distaste and rejection of us at the Political Study Centre, even before we began to talk to them.[6]

Below that level, however, everything went well. The courses brought the PAP ministers into more direct contact with their civil servants, and gave the latter an opportunity to talk frankly to them.

Then, business houses expressed an interest in the centre because they wanted to know what was happening in Southeast Asia, to its politics and to the aspirations of the people. De Cruz was humbled when two young executives from Shell — both Oxford graduates who had studied with luminaries such as A.J.P. Taylor — said that they had never believed they would find lecturers of the same level as him.

Schools, too, began to take an interest in the courses. They invited Thomson and de Cruz to speak to Sixth Formers in particular, who would go to university later or straight into the working world. He personally undertook a three-year programme in twenty or thirty schools which had Sixth Forms. He asked the students to choose the subjects on which they wanted lectures, and gave them paper to write out their questions while he was speaking. He received more than 30,000 questions. This disproved the contention that Singapore's students were politically apathetic. Instead, "our young people are very interested. It's simply a question of helping them to develop that interest. If you don't give them an outlet, the kind of outlet that these courses provided, of course they'll never ask questions about the politics of Singapore." True, the Chinese middle school students had been radicalized by the Communists, "a party working deliberately to do that", but "the English-language students were equally interested in politics, and these lectures provided them an outlet". These lectures formed the basis of four books that he wrote — *Nationalism, Forum on Nationalism, Communism* and *Forum on Communism*. The government of Sarawak learnt about the lectures and sent its civil servants to attend them. In fact, lectures were run later in Sarawak and Sabah.[7]

The poet and playwright Robert Yeo recalls that "Gerry spoke with such passion, his spittle sometimes sprinkled the air.... He was best when he spoke about Communism.... He spoke with the utter conviction of a convert from the Communist cause he had served as journalist and unionist."[8] British-born academic Ann Wee, who settled in Singapore and whose association with Carol's family and later de Cruz goes back decades, says that the colonial civil service needed "shaking up" in independent Singapore". She considers his work for the centre to have been a period of "cooling-off from his Leftwing days". By allowing him to teach there, "the system absolved him", and he, in turn, saw his work there as "the best way to serve Singapore". Indeed, de Cruz was the "heart and soul" of the centre.[9]

Former President, S.R. Nathan, a civil servant at the time he first met de Cruz in the early 1960s, remembers him as a "very gregarious person who could talk to everybody and was full of life". What made him credible in his work at the centre was that "he had belonged to the other side and he had left". It was a time when some civil servants thought that "they had to be neutral and should not get involved in the political side of the administration". But de Cruz and Thomson argued that they showed what the communists were doing to undermine the system in order to achieve power. "And if they succeeded, there would be no question of civil service neutrality. They were able to impress on us this particular fact that we could not afford to be aloof." De Cruz, being knowledgeable about "communist semantics", could read a statement and say what it really meant.[10]

Then, in 1969, Goh Keng Swee closed down the Political Study Centre. "Why? I've never found out. And George Thompson, if he knew, has never told me."[11] It was closed down because it was deemed to have achieved its purpose.[12]

THE THINKER

Papers

Gerald de Cruz's notes in his Papers bear testimony to the deep study that he put into his lectures and the wide range of issues he examined as he sought to place Singapore in the trajectory of political ideas.

His notes on Greek political thought focus on the golden years from 750 BC to 350 BC and place Plato in the context of times when the old hereditary aristocratic leadership, its power eroded by the consequences of trade, had been replaced by the tyrants or dictators, who ended governance by tradition and religious sanctions, till they in turn had been supplanted by democratic parties established in Athens and the states it dominated. Athens, vibrantly changeable, democratic, individualist and commercial; and Sparta, static, oligarchic, militarized and disciplined, represented the two poles of the argument between democracy, or rule by citizens, and oligarchy, rule by a few. "There is a parallel with Singapore", de Cruz writes, "in that most of the Greek states as a seagoing people depended on trade; commerce means fluid capital allowing men to change their place in society, and it brings men into touch with other societies, and through contact comes contrast, agricultural comparison and change.... [It] is only when men's political ideas do not seem to suit the changing facts of a changing society, that men ask political questions. And this is clearly represented by the Greeks."[13]

De Cruz acknowledges that classical Greek thinking has its limitations today. For example, the Greeks accepted slavery as the basis of their agriculture; the role of the citizen was a full-time duty that could not be reconciled with mercantile interests; and women were excluded from public life. Nevertheless, the Greeks invented the vocabulary — democracy and tyranny being the two most prominent terms — which the modern world continues to use. One reason for the longevity of the Greek experience is that they "saw political problems in terms of moral judgement";[14] the state was not just a natural necessity, but a moral necessity essential to the good life of citizens. Thus, they did not ask only what society was, but what a good society was; they did not ask only why societies had come into being, but why they should continue. Having said that, "though we use their vocabulary, their words mean different things to us, for words, through human history, gather new associations and experiences which change their meanings". An obvious example is the term "democracy", which today means representative democracy, but to the Greeks meant direct democracy — a meeting of all the citizens.[15]

Drawing on how the Greeks visualized the relationship between individual interests and social organization, de Cruz observes that each society must seek a balance between the two, dependent on time and circumstances. Following a discussion of the aristocratic and anti-democratic bent of Plato's thinking in the *Republic*, which lends itself to a justification of totalitarianism, and an analysis of his ideal of the philosopher-king, de Cruz narrows down the legacy of Platonic idealism in politics to three key issues. These are whether, in the absence of military or economic crises, any group can claim to have the correct solution; who is to decide this claim; and whether being right gives a group the moral authority to carry out its vision if it gains political power.[16] De Cruz's break with Communism, the ideological origins of whose totalitarian slant could be traced back to the praetorian elements of Plato's ideal republic, put him on guard against utopias that made existential claims on the allegiance of the masses. His reservations are clear in these notes, and they underwrite his expectations of the democratic socialism that Singapore was trying to build.

By contrast with his reservations about Platonic ideas, de Cruz's empathy with the insurrectionary aims of the English Revolution comes through clearly in his lecture notes. He acknowledges that the disturbance in thought and action caused by the seventeenth-century parliamentary revolution, like the American Revolution in the eighteenth century, has been muted by the passage of time, leading such revolutions to appear less important than contemporary revolutions. Indeed, the legacy of past revolutions has become conservative because society has internalized their lessons so well. However, the seventeenth- and eighteenth-century revolutions made fundamental points about the basis of society, they divided people to the extent of provoking war among them, and they left Britain and America fundamentally and permanently changed. They remain important today.

The English Revolution was about the control and sharing of authority. It had three aspects. In religion, it involved the Puritan revolution, which encouraged man to be his own priest and enjoy a direct approach to God. In politics, it involved the parliamentary revolution, in which man was to share power with the monarch. In economics, it involved building a pathway to the Industrial Revolution by emphasizing that man had the right to use his skills and opportunities, and only an agreed share of the fruits of his labour was to be transferred to the state for agreed purposes.[17] De Cruz analyses the complex intermingling of these three aspects of the English Revolution by referring to Max Weber's *The Protestant Ethic and the Spirit of Capitalism*, R.H. Tawney's *Religion and the Rise of Capitalism*, and the approach adopted by the great historian Christopher Hill. Essentially, the Puritan discipline corresponded with the interests of the men of capital because religious grace and economic success were considered rewards for moral virtue and economic endeavour. Unlike the mediaeval Church, Puritanism saw profit as a sign of reward and left each person to determine the morality of his economic actions. The notes mention archly that Protestant England compared well with Spain, where religious festivals accounted for 150 holidays a year![18]

However, de Cruz is clear about the political limitations of the Protestant economic settlement. He avers that the English Revolution was not a revolution by or in the name of the people, as were the American and French revolutions. The English Revolution was a "limited revolution" by a "limited class" for its "limited interests", and its revolutionary direction was thwarted when it challenged the balance of economic power *between* classes and not only *within* a class. Indeed, the congruence of landed and commercial interests in England blunted the confrontation between the feudal and bourgeois dimensions of society which made the French Revolution explosive. Nevertheless, he observes, drawing a parallel with the Magna Carta, once a revolution manages to establish universal political principles, it cannot be confined to serving the exclusive interests of the particular class or classes which launched it. So it was with the English

Revolution, in which the changing economic and political context of Stuart England led to the Civil War of 1642 and the execution of Charles I in 1649. De Cruz pays close attention to the career of Oliver Cromwell as it moved from Left to Right, and marks his transition from the leader of the parliamentary revolution to the despotic embodiment of a new status quo. The notes record compassionately the subaltern voices of the Levellers and the Diggers, stifled by the parliamentary conservatism that had succeeded monarchical absolutism. These segments of English society, which had launched the revolution within the revolution, were overtaken by events that culminated in the Restoration of the monarchy in 1660. But the English Revolution that had produced a Parliament of merchants and landowners provided the workers of England an instrument with which to establish their power in the centuries to come.

De Cruz's notes on Thomas Hobbes, John Locke and Jean Jacques Rousseau draw into the arena of political thinking insights that he gained from his analysis of historical change in England. Hobbes' classic pronouncements on the state of nature and the nature of the state, for example, were made against the background of the Civil War. To Hobbes, men are naturally quarrelsome because they compete for gain and they are diffident because of their lack of security and their quest for glory. Hence, they are in a perpetual condition of war against other men unless they submit to the authority of a common power. In the state of war, Hobbes observes unforgettably, there is no place for industry or navigation, no "culture of the earth", no account of time, no arts, no letters, no society; instead, there is the constant fear and danger of violent death; and the life of man is "solitary, poor, nasty, brutish and short". In such circumstances, men make a contract with one another to set up the state — the Leviathan or great monster — to which they surrender their powers because they would go to war if they were to retain any powers. The state is not bound by the contract, but Leviathan's appetite is limited, unlike the uncontrollable violence prevailing in the state of war. Pessimistic but intensely realistic, the frightening vision of Hobbes resonates in de Cruz's quiet and non-sensational recreation of it in his notes.[19]

However, de Cruz goes on to juxtapose against Hobbes' vision the contradictory worldview of Locke. Like Hobbes, Locke begins from nature, but his nature is informed by reason, which teaches men that they should not harm one another, because they are equal and independent. Nature provides men with a state of freedom in which to order their actions and dispose of their possessions as they deem fit, within the bounds of the law of nature, without depending on the will of others or seeking permission from them. In this liberal view, advanced by Locke, men who submit to one ruler, who is the judge in his own case, are worse off than they were in the state of nature because they have given up the right of self-defence that they enjoyed. For Hobbes, any government is better than no government, or anarchy. For Locke, the absence of government is preferable to bad government. To him, men form the state by their own consent to better define and enforce their rights by law; thus, they can withdraw that consent if the purpose is not fulfilled. Power to make laws resides in the legislative body, but it can act only as a trustee and not arbitrarily. It cannot possess more legitimate power than men had in the state of nature because, in that case, men would be in a worse condition than they were in the state of nature. The executive must be subordinate to the legislative body. Essentially, the state is both subordinate to its citizens and is limited in scope; obedience to the government is conditional; and a residual right to revolution remains.[20] De Cruz translates these issues into Singapore terms, wondering rhetorically what would happen if the government and the police were to disappear. Would Singapore follow Locke's logic?[21]

In like vein, de Cruz compares the France of Rousseau, marked by a divorce between the dominant ideas of intellectuals and contemporary institutions, "a classic situation for revolution"; with colonial societies, where "intellectuals cannot find consistency between their political ideas and the essentially non-political colonial institutions".[22] Rousseau's contribution to political thought lay in stating the political problem, not as a fact of power but of the morality of power. Legitimate rule presupposes a social group with a common purpose which the government serves, rather than a mob of isolated individuals who need to be kept in order. Rousseau's celebrated social contract does not oblige men to give anything away but to make a profitable bargain, wherein, in his inimitable characterization, peril and uncertainty are exchanged for security, natural independence for true liberty, the power of injuring others for personal safety, and the strength of personal right (always at the mercy of others' contending strength) for invincible collective strength. Given this bargain, men cannot contract out of their social obligations; they cannot live in the community for some purposes but not for others. Rousseau's general will is not the will of all but the will of men thinking of the general good. This logic, de Cruz comments, leads to "one of the most explosive phrases in political thought" — Rousseau's declaration that "it may be necessary to compel a man to be free" in that whoever refuses to obey the general will should be constrained by his fellow-citizens to do so.[23] In this postulation, Rousseau returns to the Greek concept of freedom as the freedom to be good or moral and live up to the calling of one's civic self. In being free, man leaves the state of nature and achieves civic liberty — akin to a religious conversion.

Even though he describes Rousseau's thinking succinctly, de Cruz opposes the apotheosis of the state in Rousseau. Rousseau's logic assumes that there is a generally agreed standard of goodness, and that it is expressed and enforced by the state. This, de Cruz denies, noting that it would mean that the state knows better than the individual what is good for him; government for the people would be government, not by the people but by those who know what is good for the people. Moreover, to make the state coextensive with an individual's civic freedom is to ignore the element of force that has contributed to the formation of states.[24] Then, if the general will is only an idea, a minority can seize it to make a moral claim on the behalf of the immoral exercise of power — a real danger because Rousseau concedes that a minority thinking in terms of the general good can claim to express the general will.

Nevertheless, de Cruz concludes by reiterating the call to public office inherent in Rousseau's celebration of the general will. The state is lost as soon as a man believes that its affairs do not concern him. "This is the primacy of politics as practised by Mao Tse-Tung and Nkrumah. And in our Singapore history, there can be no doubt that Singapore was more constantly politically self-conscious during the Malaysian referendum campaign than ever before."[25] In an aside touching on the importance of culture in the formation of the general will, de Cruz notes the importance of overcoming obstacles created by manners, customs and opinions in mobilizing people in new states being created in the wake of the departure of colonialism. "This is our problem in Singapore in inculcating multi-racial attitudes", he writes. Adapting the English saying that the Battle of Waterloo was won on the playing fields of Eton, he remarks that the battle of Singapore is "being won or lost" on school playgrounds. "If there the bully prevails, the secret society bully will prevail in the future. If at play time, the communities segregate themselves, so will they separate in adult life. Singapore 20 years hence is already visible in the playgrounds of today."[26]

De Cruz's lecture notes on the American Revolution of 1776 begin by underlining the importance of religious tolerance to the interests of a trading nation — "an axiom no less relevant in Singapore today".[27] The larger point he makes is that the Puritan influence accented the sense of realism in American thinking which was to define the character of their revolution. Its causes were material: The thirteen colonies of the United Kingdom had been subordinated to the interests of British mercantilism; a conflict of basic interests arose with the attempt to restrict the colonies' maritime commerce and their expansion into the hinterland; and an established landed and commercial class was present to lead the conflict. These economic causes were linked to the political revolution through the cry of "no taxation without representation", which had been a demand in the English Revolution as well. The link was personified in the landed and commercial class, which believed in doctrines of social contract and possessed an interest in public life. This class was supported by a solid middle class that maintained social and political stability during the revolution. That stability persisted in the face of differences between the established landed and commercial interests of the old settlements and the new men of the frontier.[28] The genius of the American Revolution, as of all revolutions, lay in the way in which particular issues of taxation or trade regulation or representation provoked fundamental questions about the ends of governance, the nature of sovereignty, or the meaning of freedom. De Cruz traces the course of the revolution as it unfolded through the meeting of the Continental Congress in Philadelphia, the passage of Virginia's Bill of Rights, and the Declaration of Independence. He notes how thoroughly American the American Revolution was, combining as it did the intellectual inheritance of the European Enlightenment, the fruits of the political progress made in England, and the concrete experience of Americans in their own chapter of English history.[29] He draws attention to the fact that the American Constitution was designed, not to enforce activity on the government, "as in the new states today", but to set up an inactive government that would not interfere with their individual activities and social patterns. Indeed, Americans expressly prohibited their new government from carrying out many of the activities which they had cited in justification of their revolt against Britain.[30] De Cruz goes on to discuss the role of the Civil War in the formation of American political society. He makes the pointed observation that Malaysia might have survived longer than it did had its "basic necessities and problems" been argued within its constituent states in the spirit of discussions among the thirteen sovereign ex-colonies from 1776 to 1787.[31]

De Cruz notes a direct link between the American Revolution and the French Revolution of 1789. France's failure to raise taxes from the aristocracy and wealthy members of the *parlements*, to cover the deficit caused by its support of the American colonies, compelled Louis XVI to call the Estates-General, a move which led to the revolution. At the intellectual level, French support for the American Revolution brought the latter's ideals back home in an atmosphere charged with anti-monarchical sentiment and the resentment of the professional, industrial and commercial middle class against the feudal aristocracy. Royal absolutism, epitomized by Louis XIV, had lost its capacity to seize the public imagination, and political and social institutions could not reflect the aspirations of the new classes. The storming of the Bastille on 14 July 1789, marked the victory of the Parisian working class over absolutism and tyranny.[32] De Cruz goes on to show how the

1792 war against hostile foreign nations wedded the revolution to nationalism. The success of the People's Armies against the professional invading armies cemented the relationship, which expressed the new democratic mood as well when the royal family was executed for complicity in aiding the foreign enemies of France. The ascension of the Jacobin Robespierre and the Reign of Terror — with Robespierre himself being executed — showed how revolution devours its children, but the rise of Napoleon carried the national-revolutionary idea across Europe. Although the French Revolution did not consolidate itself in a new style or theory of governance, as in the case of the American and Bolshevik revolutions, its major achievement was the abolition of the feudal system and hereditary privileges.

In accompanying lecture notes, de Cruz registers the conservative backlash to the French Revolution in the works of Edmund Burke, a British Member of Parliament of Irish origin. Although aligned with the relatively liberal attitudes of the Whigs, who sought to curtail the power of the monarchy along the lines of possibility created by the "Glorious Revolution" of 1688, Burke was upset sufficiently with the French Revolution to break with his Whig friends. He launched a scathing attack on the revolution for its total contempt of ancient institutions, including the nobility, and its intellectual celebration of violence. He relates with horror the capture of the King and the Queen, escorted from Versailles to Paris. In the same lecture notes, de Cruz summarizes the republican Tom Paine's rejoinder to Burke, in which he asks why the conservative politician should bemoan the fate that befell the Queen when he has no compassion for those who lead the most wretched of lives in the most miserable of prisons. Paine's radical justification of the rights of man, both reasoned and impassioned, stands in sharp contrast to Burke's patrician clinging to an age of supposed order and presumed nobility that the French Revolution had consigned to history.[33]

De Cruz's notes on his lectures on *The Communist Manifesto* focus on the need to understand it in the context of the revolutions of 1789, 1830, 1848, 1870, 1905 and 1917. He disagrees fundamentally with Marx's assertion that class struggles explain history, and observes that Chinese historians and philosophers point to cooperation as holding the key of history. "Marx's historical materialism is out of date", he avers, adding that dialectical materialism must contend with the reality that cognition in natural sciences is subjective, to say nothing of human society.[34] Examining why the revolutions of 1830, 1848 and 1870 had been unsuccessful, Lenin, in one of his significant contributions to Marxism, created the idea of the "professional revolutionary" as the leader who could pave the way for a successful revolution.[35] Moving on to his contemporary times, de Cruz compared old and new forms of communism. The old regime was characterized by Stalinist terror, with the secret police used to monitor society and purge the party; in the new dispensation, there was less police terror after de-Stalinization, action was not taken on a mass scale, and, in Maoist China, mass rectification campaigns and the Cultural Revolution had replaced the secret police. Likewise, Stalinist prohibitions on freedom of thought had mellowed into tolerance of criticism, debate and rethinking in European communism, although the infallibility of the dictator remained a motif of the Chinese political scene even after the departure of Stalinism in the Soviet Union. It was in China as well that the adoration of Mao's thought persisted, whereas European communism had turned towards a collegiate system after Stalin. Globally, the Soviet Union's uncompromising stance against imperialism, destined to go to war against socialism and lose, had been replaced with a strategy of peaceful coexistence with the West in the nuclear age. Although Maoism retained a stridently militant global strategy, Chinese military thinking was cautious. Also, the hard and monolithic nature of Moscow-centric Communism had become multipolar with the emergence of Beijing, Belgrade, Bucharest, Budapest, Prague and Pyongyang as autonomous centres of Communist internationalism. Correspondingly, the erstwhile Communist denunciation of countries such as India, Egypt and Indonesia for being lackeys of imperialism had been leavened by the acknowledgement that the level of state economic planning in these countries was a step towards socialist planning. The widening of geographical horizons was reflected in the intellectual sphere as well, with East European Communist states, West European Communist parties and Maoism contributing to great philosophical ferment over the assessment of Marxist fundamentals. Domestically, changing Communist systems paid more attention to consumer demands and tried to incentivize managers and workers by tying their bonuses to profits and not production per se. The encouragement of tourism and relaxation of controls on travel abroad accompanied the liberalization of life in Communist countries.[36]

Turning to the Fabian Society, de Cruz's Papers begin by making the point that the Fellowship of the New Life movement in which it originated was a utopian society since social change was to be brought about by perfecting the character of the individual. However, the "genteel, middle-class Fabians read Marx with interest but disavowed his views from the very first page". They were disillusioned by the failure of demonstrations by the unemployed in 1886 and 1887.

> It was to them a grim and exciting time what with hunger marches, parades of the workless meeting in Hyde Park and

> Trafalgar Square, and riotous clashes with the police. Bernard Shaw himself was present at a few of these clashes and noticed how a small group of trained men, the police, were able to scatter a mob overwhelmingly more numerous than themselves.
>
> As a result of their observations even left-wing Fabians decided that the Unemployed could not make a revolution. "These unhappy people," one of them wrote, "are NOT the people to make a political revolution, or even to carry through a great reform. The revolt of the empty stomach ends at the baker's shop."[37]

Instead, the Fabian Society issued a number of tracts between 1889 and 1891 that contained reformist demands. Among them were the extension of democracy and the improvement of the machinery of democratic government; the extension of government powers to improve community welfare, especially that of the working class; and government action to promote equality. De Cruz highlights the political potential of these reforms. For example, the demand that Members of Parliament and other governing bodies be paid and that election expenses be borne by the state was meant to ensure the full participation of the working class in affairs of the state and prevent the corruption that came with individuals having to finance their bid for political office. Fabians called for the prevention of "sweated labour" and for greater government participation in housing, health, education and poor relief. They supported trade union demands for an eight-hour day, and advocated local government finding jobs for the unemployed. These calls went to the heart of their concerns for the masses. In a similar vein, they called for the nationalization of the railways, canals and coalmines, and the municipalization of the water and gas supplies, docks, markets and tramways. Expressing approval for compulsory education, they demanded that it be made free and that poor children be provided with one good meal a day. Also, a "scholarship ladder" should be made available to poor students. Heavy taxation of unearned incomes, a steeply progressive income tax rate and high death duties would help bridge the economic gulf in society. Turning to the Fabian demand for political equality for women, de Cruz recalls the interesting principle behind it. The principle was that men no longer needed special privileges to protect them against women, and therefore the sexes should enjoy equal political rights. "I tend to think that those sardonic words could only have been written by Bernard Shaw."[38]

De Cruz contrasts the Fabian and Marxist approaches to socialism. He points out that the Fabians used the term "class" in very much the same way that Marx did — "broad groupings of the people defined strictly in terms of ownership, or non-ownership of the means of production" — and accepted that there was a serious conflict of interest between the classes. "What they denied was the Marxist contention that it is through the class-struggle and class-war that we shall bring socialism into existence.... To the Marxist doctrine of the inevitability of revolution, they opposed the concept of the inevitability of gradualness, of evolution into socialism. Their function, they felt, was to make this transition a conscious one on the part of the workers. They were certain too that, in Britain at least, it would be a peaceful transition, while recognising that in other countries, where democratic institutions were absent, it might not be."[39] De Cruz criticises Fabian doctrine for never having reached the "highest level of theoretical originality", but he commends the group for its deep concern with facts, detailed research, clarity of presentation, and the cool and rational atmosphere in which their arguments sought to appeal to the professional and administrative classes. With the formation of the Labour Party, Fabian ideas came to have a profound influence on the lives and destinies of the British people.

Taking stock, de Cruz avers: "It is true that the river of political opinion in Britain has flowed in a direction which the Fabians approved, but it has not run into Socialism. It is still a moot question whether the river will go on in this desired direction or whether it has already emptied itself into the Welfare State."

Elsewhere, however, de Cruz suggests that history has not ended. In an essay, "The Conflict of Generations", he speaks of a new world "struggling to be born". Humanity was participating in the "fourth act in the creation of the modern world".[40] The first three were the political, industrial and technological revolutions; now the world was witnessing the cultural revolution. A "multi-religious, multi-cultural and multi-lingual society of human beings, living in creative tension and dialogue across the face of the earth, is for the first time in our history, a concrete possibility".[41] In this context, the conflict of generations is but natural given the thirst of the young for change. "The young, being idealistic, are often on the front-lines of idealistic causes: they want to stop war; they want equal rights for all members of society, irrespective of ethnic ancestry, sex or creed; they want the abolition of corruption and the removal of corrupt leaders; they want the liberation of their countries from foreign rule. When peaceful methods fail, violence breaks out."[42] In a speech to young Singaporeans, de Cruz does not support the use of violence, but calls on his audience repeatedly to embrace the Socratic injunction that the unexamined life is not worth living. Commenting on the social role of intellectuals and elites, he commends the artist for possessing "the power of sympathy, a sympathy that can penetrate into the lives of the ordinary people, into the lives of all people and understand what is happening to them".[43]

One conclusion that de Cruz draws from his extensive commentaries on political theories and processes is Singapore's need for an ideology. "This is an ideological world and without an ideology of our own the vacuum might be filled by one which is hostile to us", he writes in his Papers. "An ideology motivates, sustains and justifies us in the long pull ahead. It fills in the gaps and inspires us in our most difficult passage. Above all, an ideology is comprehensive, and therefore unites us despite all the differences that tend to keep us apart from one another." Admittedly, ideologies can be jealously exclusive and they should not become ends in themselves. Thus, in a newly independent country like Singapore with a plural society, "we need an ideology which reconciles, synthesises, and unit[e]s, which is forward-looking and yet can combine the best of the past to help it meet and overcome future problems".[44] De Cruz's belief in the importance of a sustaining ideology to underpin nation-building reflected the democratic socialist temper of the times in which he wrote. In spite of his rejection of communism, he remained adamant about the progressive legacy of revolutionary thinking in nation-building, invoking the historical agency of the French and Industrial revolutions for their "continuous impact" and "their normalisation of change as the outstanding feature of life".[45] For the nation as much as for the individual, the unexamined life was not worth living.

Books

Gerald de Cruz's books on nationalism and communism, which include answers to basic questions asked after his lectures, along with the accompanying forum books, which feature the more controversial questions for detailed answers, provide an excellent idea of him as a thinker. He was a deeply thoughtful man who would have excelled in an intellectual profession had he had access to a university education. But his instinctive affinity with ideas and his search for truth through the contest of ideas resulted in a natural erudition that was also earthy. In style, the books combine sharpness of observation with keen polemical vigour that reflect his intellectually combative years as a communist. Just as he had turned to communism for a home away from his Catholic home, his recantation of communism, like his earlier rejection of Catholicism, bears heavy traces of the very past that he had left behind. De Cruz sought in democratic socialism the promise of a humane religion free of the institutional strictures and the use of violence that underpinned the communist belief in justice.

Nationalism

Thus, the guiding spirit of *Nationalism*[46] is both Jacobin and Bolshevik. De Cruz traces the origins of the idea to the transformative energies of the French Revolution and the Industrial Revolution. True, he begins by celebrating nationalism as a force that has rebuffed two international challenges — imperialism and communism — and in this he is factually correct. Decolonization attests to the power of anti-colonial nationalism to fight imperialism (which itself emanated from the earlier triumph of the national idea in Europe), while the Sino-Soviet split of the 1960s revealed that national interpretations of the same ideology, Marxism-Leninism, could trump the internationalism that was central to the global reach of that ideology. Of course, nationalism was hardly an innocent among the wolves. It had not only underpinned colonial expansionism but it had also helped shape a world full of contradictions between "progress and regress, democracy and totalitarianism, liberty and concentration camps, civilization and savage, mass-murderous wars, material prosperity and squalor".[47]

Yet, the torrential force of nationalism is undeniable. Invoking Marx's insight that an idea becomes a material force when it seizes the imagination of the masses, de Cruz writes of nationalism with revolutionary fervour. "It has swept through continents and civilizations. It has wrecked forever the systems of absolute monarchy and feudalism. It has brought torment and liberation, bloody revolution and independence, despair and hope, death and a new life to countless millions."[48] "It was through the French Revolution that the Word of [the] Enlightenment was made flesh", he remarks with a deliberate touch of blasphemy.[49] The revolution spread "the conviction that people exist independently of their rulers, and there can be no lawful ruler except with the consent of the people".[50] Liberty, Equality and Fraternity summed up the mood of the age that was dawning, and the world appeared to have been born anew.[51] Everywhere in the book, de Cruz is mesmerized not only by the visceral power but also by the almost elemental scale of nationalism.

De Cruz notes a vital connection between the French Revolution and nationalism.

> By making the nation coextensive with the territory of the state, by making the nation the trustee of the sovereignty of the people, by entrusting the people, as citizens, with the defence and protection of the nation-state, the French revolution laid down the strong foundations of the nation-state, a work that continues until today, and here, and now, in our republic, our city-state of Singapore.[52]

"How much of modern society originated in the French Revolution!" he exclaims.[53]

The other source of modernity was the Industrial Revolution. Again, he writes about it with elegant exuberance. "In fact there has never been another event in modern history which has caused so much pain on the one hand, or given rise to more extraordinary vistas of progress on the other"[54] than the Industrial Revolution. He describes how "this marriage of science to need which produced the machine" was "one of the climacteric moments in human history" because it raised human productivity to levels that had been unimagined before and changed the nature of distance and the meaning of transport.[55] He describes the Industrial Revolution as being four revolutions in one. There was a mechanical revolution "which mechanized any human activity which can be broken down into separate routines". There was a revolution in mass production caused by the assembly line and the conveyor belt. The revolution in automation enabled machines to run machines through computers "at speeds faster than thought". And there was a revolution in electronics which turned individuals and countries into instant neighbours.[56]

It was the social consequences of these technological processes that concerned de Cruz the most. Feudalism had tied the villager to the land, but there had been at least relationships of reciprocity between him and the landowner. In the new, squalid and anonymous towns, however, people "come under the cold, cruel and indifferent laws of the cash nexus" where each generation has just enough to subsist on to produce the next hapless generation to take its place. But it was "this daily crucifixion" that produced in workers the awareness that their one strength lay in their numbers, and unity made numbers effective. Thus, out of the desperation of the times was born the trade union. The oppressed working class demanded, first, recognition of its humanity and, second, better pay and working conditions.[57] Trades unions soon realized that they were up against the political system as well, because laws were made to protect the rights of capital, not labour. Out of this wave of awareness were born the first political parties of the working class. Such were the developments through which the Industrial Revolution "began to add new dimensions of breadth, depth, consciousness and power to the nation".[58]

What the Industrial Revolution also did was to encourage radically transformative forces, such as education, because literacy was necessary to run machines efficiently. Widespread reading created the economic conditions for daily newspapers to flourish, and the emergence of a substantial reading public in turn created a widespread sense of the nation. A middle class emerged, "so dynamic that it rejected absorption; so confident that it looked with contempt on heredity and unearned privilege and social position".[59] The mobilization of citizens for defence gave them a collective sense of national responsibility for it — a development which de Cruz relates to the importance of National Service in Singapore.[60]

De Cruz concludes his brief but nevertheless majestic survey of nationalism with almost an ode to anti-colonial nationalism.

> The powerful, jingoistic nationalisms of the West, spilling out of their native lands in search of wealth, trade, and aggrandizement, conquered Asia and Africa and made all their dreams come true, in an orgy of war, suppression, exploitation and arrogance. In so doing they bit deep into our psyche, *sampai tulang* as we say in *bahasa kebangsaan*, and stung into awakening, giants who had long slumbered.[61]

But he warns that "arrogant and sadistic" foreign nationalism should not feed "provincial and xenophobic" indigenous nationalism.[62] Imperialism and fascism are right-wing deviations of nationalism; its two left-wing deviations are communism and democracy. He allowed communism its claim to be the dynamics of struggle in nation-building, but he preferred over it democracy, the dynamics of freedom in nation-building.[63] Answering a question included in the book, he offered developmental nationalism as a model for Singapore. This meant accepting the interdependence of modern societies, making sacrifices for the country's modernization, respecting indigenous cultural traditions but not glorifying them, and being fraternal towards others.[64] He did not have in mind any kind of cowed conformity. There was a "high place in national development" for "serious dissent" and opposition so long as they were born out of loyalty to Singapore and aimed to increase its chances of survival or strengthen its democratic structure.[65]

Forum on Nationalism,[66] the companion volume to *Nationalism*, fleshes out the ideas presented in the first book by examining the Singapore and regional contexts closely.

De Cruz warns at the outset that Singapore's multiracial make-up can threaten its national unity "if we see ourselves as Chinese, or Indian, or Malay, before we see ourselves as Singaporeans. In other words, if we put the birth-place of our ancestors before our own." Moreover, the ancestral lands of Singaporeans, such as China and India, could have a potent attraction because they possess long histories and highly developed cultures. Seeing "ourselves as Chinese or Indians first" would defeat the "vital purpose of nation-building, which is to give our undivided allegiance to the land of our birth". In the absence of that loyalty, each community would begin to vie with the others, imagine itself superior and therefore destined to rule over the others, and open the floodgates of chauvinism that would overwhelm Singapore. In that regard, enmity would follow if a community felt that its language — the most vital element of its culture — had been slighted. Hence the choice of four official languages — Chinese, Tamil, English and Malay — to acknowledge "our local reality". Hence also the adoption of Malay as the national language, to acknowledge "our regional reality". These were some of the ways to prevent cultural conflicts. "Cultures can clash, because they are different ways of experiencing the same reality", de Cruz writes.[67]

On one issue he is adamant, however: There is no place for race in nationality because there is no such thing as race! Race "is a myth"; "there is no such thing as a Chinese race, a Malay race, an Indian race, or a European race, or even a white race or a black race", he declares unequivocally, because "the differences within so-called racial groups are as large as between those groups". Hence scientists urge that the term "race" be used only in the phrase "the human race" in order to distinguish humans from other species. However, social usage lags behind science, he remarks, recalling humorously an episode at the National Library, where he wrote down "Human" against the word "Race" on the registration card. It took him a while to convince the clerk across the counter that he was not a member of the Eurasian race, since none exists. When the man finally understood what he was saying and acknowledged his membership of the human race, de Cruz assured him pithily that if he ever changed into a baboon "I will change my library card immediately".[68]

There is an interesting question on whether a Singaporean nationalism is possible given both the country's short history and the absence of a common history, traditions and experiences shared by its people. De Cruz disagrees with the question's premise. He notes that modern Singapore began in 1819, just thirty years after the French Revolution — one of the two formative events of nationalism — and so "our history as a modern nation is not as short as we sometimes feel".[69] China and India had long histories, but their people had not been citizens for long. Indeed, even in France, women received the vote in 1948, the same year that Singapore women of British-subject status won that right. In answer to another question, he says that "we have been through much together in the past 150 years, enough for a distinct Singaporean identity to emerge. Why we may sense it so keenly at the moment is because we have had only a few years as an independent people, responsible ultimately for our own destiny."[70] As for the absence of common traditions, he put this in perspective: "It is because imperialism had divided us into little compartments, and thus laid the framework for ignorance, suspicion, jealousy and hostility between the communities that we need nationalism, the sense of a common loyalty and bond, superior to the smaller allegiance to clan, community, culture or religion which tend[s] to divide us."[71] Hence, Singaporeans must not let themselves become "victims of that Imperialist-flavoured version of history which tries to make us feel inferior to Westerners. Into the dustbin with such a canard!"[72] Singapore had acted upon and modified all that the French and Industrial revolutions had contributed to the modern world, for good or ill. The currents unleashed by them had swept through the island, but they had not swept it away.

Dwelling on the theme of "developmental nationalism", he defends it in terms of the democratic socialism espoused by the People's Action Party. The origins of this socialism — with Eduard Bernstein in Germany and the Fabians in England — lay in a fervent belief in socialism as the nationalization of the means of production, distribution and exchange. But democratic socialism turned towards a mixed economy, partly private and partly nationalized, when it was confronted by the horrors of the Soviet Union's totalitarian state economy, which eliminated the rights and privileges of the working class itself. In the Singapore context, democratic socialism was also "pragmatic socialism", based on attracting both local and foreign capital to finance industrialization. Since the ambit of local capital was restricted traditionally to commerce and trade, Singapore invited in foreign capital by offering political stability, security and long-term viability. This "developmental socialism" demonstrated the government's concern for workers and the poor.[73]

On that note, de Cruz disagrees with a questioner who asks whether locating an external enemy might not be the best and quickest way of instilling nationalism. Singapore being a small country, de Cruz says, an "aggressive posture on our part towards anyone else would simply bring the world's ridicule upon us" and would be unconvincing to Singaporeans themselves, "no matter how loudly our Government shouted, or made us shout, against the alleged enemy" unless, of course, there was an imminent threat from a real enemy.[74] At the other end of the spectrum, a question on Singapore's possible re-Merger with Malaysia elicits the comment that both countries endured "one resounding failure" at Merger and might not come out of another one quite so successfully.[75]

An enigmatic question on the enemies of nationalism leads de Cruz to speak of internal and external enemies. Among the first, he mentions chauvinism, communalism, religious fanaticism and "linguistic cultism", all of which fragment the nation.[76] Another internal enemy is "the ideologue who puts his allegiance to his political party and its international image above his nation", an example being "the communists who often embark on ruinous national adventures in the cause of international communism".[77] The main external enemy is "cosmopolitanism".

> By this I mean the views of the rather idealistic, and sensitive person who says, vaguely and beautifully, that he is a citizen of the world, not of the state of Singapore, and as such he has higher ideals than those of the nation-state. The trouble with this kind of person is that although he appears to be serving the kind of ultimate ideal which all of us carry in our hearts, in fact he is merely paying lip-service to it. He is one of those extremely irresponsible persons who recognize and claim all their rights both as human beings and as citizens, but few of their duties.... One can imagine the anarchy and chaos this would result in if all of us acted in this way.[78]

Nationalism can be protected from its internal foes by educating citizens to understand that their survival depends on their commitment to the high loyalty of the nation-state. Nationalism can be protected from cosmopolitanism by teaching people that they need roots to withstand the turbulence of life, that cosmopolitanism is itself "a parasite on nationalism", and that it springs from a mistaken sense of inferiority that apes the allegedly superior ways of others. Appreciating others is one thing; it is another to be driven to "either slavish imitation of the foreign, or unjustified contempt of one's own".[79]

Extrapolating from this theme in his answer to another question, de Cruz acknowledges that Socrates said he was not a citizen of Athens but of the world. But what the great Athenian had meant was that there are "crucial times, moments of truth, when our conscience conflicts in great seriousness with the demands of the state". Then, in pursuit of freedom, justice or truth, a person thinks himself bound to oppose the demands of the state or of the nation. But this confrontation is resolved at a higher level of reality where "national and individual needs meet in their joint concern for the ultimate liberation of the human being". Indeed, the apparent confrontation ultimately "adds substance and meaning to both the human and the national record". When an individual opposes his community in spite of his loyalty to it because his conscience will accept nothing less, he imparts a "new depth" to both humanity and his nation, which will become a part of the history of his people and inspire others long after he is dead.[80]

Two questions — "If a man can be both a socialist and a nationalist can he not be both a communist and a nationalist too?" and "Can nationalism defeat communism?"[81] — draw a long, reflective answer. To the extent that communism is a universal ideology, de Cruz notes, it is supra-national, anti-national and sides with the international working-class against imperialism.

Communism denounces nationalism as being bourgeois in origin, that is, a device used by imperialists and capitalists "to turn the nationals, that is, the workers of one country, against the workers of another country, in wars which are started and encouraged by the capitalists to bring them great financial profits".[82] At the same time, however, communists very often play an integral part in the fight against imperialist or fascist rule. In Singapore under both British colonial rule before World War II and the Japanese Occupation, "the communist party was the chief, if not the only, vehicle for the nationalist aspirations and struggles of our people".[83] However, even in this phase of the nationalist struggle, when communists organize and develop an anti-imperialist and anti-fascist trade union, peasant, youth and cultural movement, they often weaken the overall movement by undermining anti-communist nationalist forces or embarking on ill-advised militancy that may spark civil war. The communist insurgency in Malaya from 1948 to 1959 offers an excellent example of the dual face of the communist role in nationalist struggles.

Of course, de Cruz adds, when communists come to power they implement the dictatorship of the proletariat, "which is really dictatorship by the leaders of the communist party", and condemn and suppress nationalistic sentiments.[84] Turning to the recent past, de Cruz notes the limitations of attempts by the international communist movement to capture the nationalist imagination in communist countries. Instead, nationalism there uses the Communist Party itself to express itself. The survival of Tito's Yugoslavia as an independent state in 1947; the Hungarian revolution of 1956 before it was crushed, though not for ever, by Soviet tanks; the Sino–Soviet split of the 1960s; and the Warsaw Pact invasion of Czechoslovakia in 1968 — all these attest to the inability of the Comintern, the monolithic communist international movement, to control national aspirations.[85]

"It certainly does look", de Cruz writes archly, "as if international communism, at the time of its great expansion, has begun to shatter itself on the rocks of nationalism".[86]

Communism

In spite of his break with communism, Gerald de Cruz is scrupulously fair to the appeal of the ideology, even as he criticizes its extravagant claims, intolerant means, totalitarian ends and horrendous excesses, all rationalized in the name of an ultimate and inevitable truth. *Communism*[87] begins with the acknowledgement that communism, like nationalism, is not only a legacy of the French and Industrial revolutions but that the four decades from the Bolshevik victory in 1917 to the launch of Sputnik in 1957 represented a period of "superlative achievement". Indeed, communism continues to provide an alternative to capitalist development when it is sabotaged by inefficiency and corruption; communism delivers the goods if people are willing to pay "the human price it extorts in pain and suffering, death and indignity, terror and concentration camps". Communism, "one of the great missionary movements of change and destiny", has propelled the Soviet Union into the ranks of the superpowers, has spread over a third of the land surface of the globe, and controls the destiny of more than a third of humankind.[88] The power of communism derives from its being "a philosophy of struggle, a party of struggle, a strategy of struggle, and a tactic of struggle".[89] Communists have shown that "they can take the most backward, unpromising and unproductive situations, fertilize them with struggle, and produce an abundant harvest of revolutionary fervour, tenacity and will".[90] He adds:

> Communism has succeeded in the economic development of hundreds of millions not because it is good or democratic, nor

> because it is ruthless or dictatorial; it has succeeded because it has been a nexus of struggle — philosophical, organizational, strategic, and tactical — all concentrated on one objective: to change the world in the image of communism and the dictatorship of the proletariat.[91]

De Cruz summarizes the main tenets of dialectical and historical materialism, noting how, by making matter the essence of nature, it denies God, religion, belief in immortality and other spiritual aspects of man. "But it does not leave the altars empty."[92] Marx replaces God with man. This was to be the basis of Marxism as perhaps the greatest of the secular religions. In place of the Christian movement from *Paradise Lost* to *Paradise Regained,* Marxism posits the journey from Asiatic tribal communism to modern scientific communism. For redemption by Jesus Christ, the Son of God, communism offers redemption by the proletariat, the Son of Man. "For the Christian, the guide and father, friend and confessor on his difficult journey through life is the Church. For the communist, the guide, father, friend and confessor in his lifelong struggle is the Communist Party."[93]

De Cruz had personal experience of transferring his affiliation from the Church to the Party. In this book, he condenses that experience into three stages of the transformation which communist cadres undergo: indoctrination, "at war" psychology, and the cell. Indoctrination means understanding ideology, which imbues the cadre with the outlook of dialectical and historical materialism. A further consequence is that the cadre believes that he is at war with all anti-communist or non-communist forces, such as capitalism or imperialism. The ends justify the means in this war. The cell's weekly meetings, usually divided into two sessions — collective accounting of one's work, and individual accounting — create a bond resembling that of the family. As cell-members critique one another, no holds are barred, "yet no criticism is made with malice".[94]

De Cruz moves on to talk of the communists' United Front strategy of allying themselves with the broad non-communist masses on the way to establishing a communist state. This is because the Communist Party is not strong enough to win a revolution in spite of its discipline and toughness.

> To overthrow a government is not easy. It needs a communist spearhead with sufficient mass support to defeat the forces ranged against them — army, police, militia, etc. The communist-type United Front strategy was developed to enable them to swing over to their side a significant proportion of the people, by impressing them with their zeal, their sincerity, their activity and their sacrifice for the cause, to make the people believe that it is the communists alone who are their real champions.[95]

The strategy allies the communists with the people's demands for the redressal of grievances over oppression, unemployment, low wages and so on. It has two variations, the soft line and the hard line. The soft line is used when communism is embryonic or weak and its supporters are estimated to form less than five per cent of the population. This line involves supporting general goals such as democracy, constitutionalism, civil liberties and legal processes. The hard line is used when the communists command the support of more than twenty per cent of the people. It sees them denouncing democracy, parliament and the law as a sham and taking to the streets, open fields and back alleys. In practice, the two lines are combined and communists use two types of apparatus — one which is legal and above-ground, and the other which is illegal and underground — to further their goals.[96] At the international level, the Communist Party of the Soviet Union advances the United Front strategy of Peaceful Coexistence, seeking to unite with anti-imperialist forces to overthrow the imperialist West by using all methods short of world war. The Chinese Communist Party, however, denounces Moscow as a lackey of Washington and proclaims its own United Front strategy of Countryside of the World *versus* Cities of the World. This strives to unite Asians, Africans and Latin Americans in a global struggle against imperialist Western Europe and Northern America, using revolutionary wars of national liberation to encircle and destroy imperialism.[97]

On balance, communists have contributed to the liberation of the world by fighting imperialism and fascism, particularly during World War II, when they organized themselves to resist and fight back the scourge, unlike other groups which were afraid or capitulated or became turncoats. They make a tremendous contribution to nation-building when they take over a state, Russia being a good example. However, the human price of communist modernization is a devastating one.[98] Internationally, the Sino–Soviet split exemplifies a struggle, not between Soviet revisionists and Chinese dogmatists, but between communism and nationalism. "It is a struggle in which international communism is being broken into fragments on the rock of the nation-state."[99]

In the book's question-and-answer section, de Cruz talks about the relationship between communism and democratic socialism. Both ideologies believe that "political democracy is anaemic without economic justice", are pledged to "the abolition of capitalist exploitation of the worker for the sake of private profit", believe in a classless society, and agree that humans have a right to equal opportunities.[100] However, communists describe their socialism as scientific and brand democratic socialism as being revisionist — a charge which its pioneers accepted proudly because "revisionism belongs to the very essence of the scientific method".[101] They disagreed with the communist prediction of the "inevitable, imminent and apocalyptic collapse of capitalism", maintaining that capitalists could learn to avoid repeating their errors. As early as the 1890s, democratic socialists had used accumulating evidence to disprove the Marxist prophesy that Britain, France, Germany and the United States would be the first to become communist because their advanced capitalist structures had brought them into closer proximity to the collapse of capitalism and the onset of communism.[102] Democratic socialists also came into conflict with communists over the methods necessary to establish a classless society. Democratic socialists were opposed to the violent overthrow of the state and the installation of the dictatorship of the proletariat, maintaining that it was absurd to replace a capitalist dictatorship with a communist one because the masses would be equally victims of either. This is exactly what occurred after the Russian Revolution, where the ruthless destruction of capitalist and feudal institutions did not lead to democracy but to "a totalitarian economy and polity within the framework of a police state" and the "dictatorship of the Communist Party".[103] Indeed, Stalin's Red terror and other examples of the

> unedifying spectacle of communism in action led the democratic socialists to modify their views on the necessity for the total nationalization of all the means of production, distribution and exchange. They realized that nationalization on this scale, merging state and employer into one gargantuan entity, would render the worker more helpless than ever before in his struggle for justice and for a higher standard of living.[104]

Contemporary democratic socialism is pragmatic and oriented to answering the diverse priorities of different countries. The economy should blend the public and private sectors so that they could check and balance each other, although the major instruments of production, distribution and exchange should lie in public hands.[105]

Forum on Communism,[106] the accompanying book to *Communism*, begins with an insightful analysis of why communism is not suitable for Singapore. First, trade, Singapore's lifeline, is almost entirely in private hands. It would be a victim of a terrible confrontation between the government and the trading community in a communist Singapore, resulting finally in the virtual elimination of the city's status as one of the world's great ports. Secondly, communist industrialization would be financed by the implementation of laws designed to enforce the highest possible rate of savings for the purposes of investment. The existing use of capital, aid and expertise drawn from different sources would cease, given the Malayan Communist Party's total support for China in its conflict with both the capitalist West and the Soviet Union. Thirdly, the denial of personal liberties and the suspension of the rule of law, dramatized by the monstrosities of the Japanese Occupation, would inflict immense individual and social pain on people. Fourthly, neither Malaysia nor Indonesia would tolerate a communist Singapore because that would entail their greatest port falling into the hands of their greatest enemy. The two countries would intervene swiftly and massively in Singapore, the communist government would not be able to count on the loyalty of the army, and Singapore would be subjugated. Fifthly, a takeover of Singapore, a predominantly Chinese state in an overwhelmingly Malay neighbourhood, by a largely Chinese communist party affiliated to China, would legitimate suspicions of Singapore as a third China. Singapore would be attacked and ethnic Chinese in the region would be massacred, pushing back racial integration for one or more generations. Sixthly, the communists were interested, not in capturing Singapore exclusively, but Malaya as well.[107] Hence the impossibility of legalizing the Communist Party. It had been legal in Singapore and West Malaysia between 1945 and 1948, but that year it took to the jungles and had remained since then in a state of armed revolt against the democratically elected governments of independent Singapore and Malaysia.[108]

Turning to communist propaganda, de Cruz devotes two pages of the book to discussing how the pro-communist Barisan Sosialis used education to further its goals in the kindergartens it ran. Children between the ages of three and six were taught to colour drawings that bore little relation to Singapore. For example, there was a drawing of a little boy with fist clenched sitting astride a prostrate American soldier, the caption exhorting him to strike American soldiers till they are dead. Another picture showed a child in soldier's uniform with a rifle slung over his shoulder; the child marches off to the caption that describes him as belonging to the children's Liberation Army. These books bear the publisher's imprint, Barisan Sosialis Malaya, along with the party's full address and two telephone numbers. The methods used to teach numerals in these kindergartens was even more subversive, de Cruz notes. In book One, the numeral "6" is illustrated by six lanterns carrying the slogan, "Long Live Chairman Mao". A drawing depicting the shooting down of eight American planes illustrates "8"; "9" is shown by a drawing of nine guerrillas carrying sub-machine guns; and "10" by the destruction of a truck carrying that number of American soldiers. Book Three transports the young minds into the arena of the guerrilla war waged against the United States. It is full of drawings depicting the destruction of American soldiers, aircraft and helicopters. Elsewhere, the Americans are shown in abject surrender, while the guerrillas and Red Guards are triumphant. There are also derogatory pictures of the Prime Minister of Singapore and the former Prime Minister of Malaysia.[109]

Answering a question on why Mao's *Red Book* is banned in Singapore but not in countries such as the United States or Britain, de Cruz says that it is one of the foremost weapons of the Cultural Revolution. "To allow it in Singapore then would be to allow a spearhead of today's communist Chinese revolution to pierce our social fabric. We cannot allow that under present circumstances — unlike Britain and America, where indeed the *Red Book* has become something of a best-seller too — because our mass base is Chinese."[110] He reiterates a larger point linking politics to ethnicity:

> Perhaps the single most important element in our survival is to prove that the Singapore Chinese are Singaporeans first; that this island is not and never will become a third China; that we are not an alien Chinese enclave in the heart of Southeast Asia; that we are true Singaporeans and Southeast Asians, owing our undivided loyalty and allegiance to Singapore and to this region. Anything less would be disastrous, not only for us, but also for the rest of Southeast Asia, because all the countries in this region have plural societies with substantial Chinese minorities.[111]

To allow the *Red Book* would be to encourage local communists, who take their directions from Beijing, and encourage Chinese nationals such as seamen who arrive at the port to march through Singapore waving the *Red Book* and chanting the thoughts of Mao. One Chinese seaman actually tried to do this.

Speaking of Vietnam, de Cruz returns to the Singapore scene. He does not believe that a communist Vietnam would communize Southeast Asia. Not only would a unified Vietnam face the massive challenge of reconstruction after the war, but also, it would be likely to adopt a nationalist posture towards China, much as Yugoslavia, Hungary and Czechoslovakia had done vis-à-vis the Soviet Union. Moreover, with the Indonesian Communist Party virtually destroyed, no communist party was in a position to use the success of communism in Vietnam to gain power and threaten the region. In Malaysia and Burma, communist uprisings had been put down decisively. Singapore, on its part, had been so successful in reducing the appeal of communism that communists and pro-communists had turned their attention to brainwashing kindergarten children. "To pervert the minds of children between the ages of three and six is not a pleasant occupation, but the fact that they are doing this probably goes to show that they too believe that the victory of communism in Singapore is not closer than at least one generation away!"[112]

A question on the Cultural Revolution sees de Cruz tracing it to the failure of China's Great Leap Forward and the rural communes between 1958 and 1960, which placed a great strain on the leadership of the Chinese Communist Party. More pragmatic party leaders, who formed an overwhelming majority in the Politburo of the Central Committee, wanted to halt Mao's ideological adventurism. His control of the party now under pressure, Mao branded these leaders revisionists and right-wing opportunists who would follow the Soviet Union in leading China down the capitalist path of American lackeyism. He launched the Cultural Revolution to purge these traitorous bourgeois cadres along with intellectuals who had become steadily more disaffected with him. His weapon was not the army but the Red Guards. The guerrilla days, and the revolutionary peasant movement in Hunan in particular, had demonstrated to him the effectiveness of a spearhead which "would be able to dramatize the revolution, create the atmosphere of revolution, the cries, the shouts, the slogans, the banging on the drums, the action, the condemnation, the cathartic wave sweeping through town and village, sweeping away all the old and evil capitalist remnants — a spearhead of revolution-makers, learning how to make revolutions by making revolutions".[113] Mao found his weapon in millions of students. The Red Guards did indulge in acts of hooliganism, but they were more than the hooligans that many anti-communists had made them out to be.

> They are an immense, youthful and zealous army who have fulfilled many roles: as spearhead of the revolution; as creators of true revolutionary fervour; as future leaders of China bathing themselves in revolutionary purpose and action in order to become genuine leaders of the permanent revolution; as a task force extraordinary which mobilized the enthusiasm, energy and puritanical force of youth to hit the enemies of Mao in a hundred different places at the same time...[114]

They were also the screen behind which the real power-play was taking place between Mao, Lin Biao and the People's Liberation Army (PLA), on the one hand; and Liu Shaoqi, who had replaced Mao as China's President, the Chinese Communist Party, and some elements of the PLA, on the other.

In 1969, the third year of the Cultural Revolution, Zhou Enlai declared it should be wound up, and Mao's publicists declared that the revisionists had been routed completely. In de Cruz's assessment, Mao's victory was not as clear-cut as that. After all, Mao's isolation in the party had been revealed when he could find no one but his wife, Jiang Qing, to lead the revolution. However, de Cruz disagrees with facile critics of the revolution, noting that that tumultuous phase in Chinese history reflected the difficulty, not only of ruling 700 million people, and not only of feeding that poor and backward populace which was made up overwhelmingly of peasants, but of placing the nation on the path of industrial development. Mao fell back on the one method that he knew and had used to superb effect: guerrilla strategy for the people's war. "Can anyone blame Mao for trying to adopt the successful strategies of wartime to the battle for industrial and agricultural development?"[115] But he was up against problems at the heart of the party revolving around cadres who were guilty of corruption, abuse of power, disobedience and apathy, and who could behave with impunity because citizens could not limit their power. Drastic measures were needed to overhaul the party, even if this meant dismantling it. "This I think accounts for the religious fervour of the Cultural Revolution."[116] However, de Cruz suggests that while fervour is a necessary ingredient of the march of change, it is not a sufficient one. Contrasting China's and India's food problems, he points out that communist China used almost all its foreign earnings to buy wheat from Canada and Australia, two capitalist countries. By contrast, India, a democracy, has made tremendous progress in agriculture "since being relieved of the British incubus".[117] But in both cases, the real problem was not food production as much as rapid population growth.

In the concluding section of the book, "Conflict in Communism",[118] de Cruz returns to the theme of nationalism and communism. "Ideologies do not only unite; they also tend to divide, particularly when they are draped over the structure of the nation-state."[119] If communism is to succeed in conquering the world, it must have a global strategy in which one communist nation-state will have to be accepted as the leader. That role had fallen on Russia in 1917 for the simple reason that it was the first communist nation-state and its national interests had coincided with its ideological objectives. But with the spread of the ideology, other communist nation-states had come into being, and, in order to maintain their legitimacy among their own populations, they had to further national interests that did not coincide necessarily with those of the Soviet Union. The Soviet Union was a Eurasian land mass but a European power; China, oriented towards Asia, saw itself as the natural leader of a global communist movement whose storm centres lay in Asia, Africa and Latin America. The ideological analyses of the global situation advanced by Moscow and Beijing rationalized their divergent national positions within the international communist movement. However, de Cruz cautioned against democratic triumphalism over the Sino–Soviet split, although it had divided international communism by fracturing many local communist parties into pro-Moscow and pro-Beijing factions. The very fact that communism was capable of being modified along national lines while remaining a global movement showed its adaptability to change and thus its vitality as a totalitarian alternative to democracy. In the circumstances, the best course for democratic countries — which, too, had been rocked by the protests of the 1960s — would be to reform their own institutions. Moreover, many underdeveloped countries faced problems of hunger, population explosion and ethnic tensions. Instead of gloating over divisions in the communist world, it would be better to build more bridges of trade, education and culture between the democratic and communist worlds. Both would have to adapt to changes taking place within and without.

Democracy

De Cruz answers several questions on democracy in the periodical, *Prospect.*[120] He begins by noting that no country on earth practises pure democracy. Instead, like other human institutions, democracy is an inevitable part of historical change and varies in structure and substance from place to place. However, democracy should be representative, limited, constitutional and rotatory. Representation means that citizens should be able to choose their government through free and secret elections in an atmosphere where opposition parties exist, grow and eventually flourish. Limitation means that the government's powers are limited through the separation of powers among the executive, the legislature and the judiciary, unlike in a dictatorship, where one group monopolizes power. Constitutionalism means, with the exception of Britain, that the written constitution is the supreme law and protects basic rights. Rotation involves the government surrendering its powers of rule every few years in elections. Together, these requirements make democracy a tool to preserve as much freedom as possible in special situations and conditions.[121]

Churchill famously said that democracy is the worst form of government except for every other system. De Cruz elaborates on this by arguing that all systems of government are defective because the individual often feels poorly done by the need to regulate the behaviour of man in society. The growth in population, the increasing bureaucratization of administration, and social anonymity increase the individual's sense of helplessness. Revolts taking place in democratic societies are protests against an insufficiently responsive democratic structure. But, he goes on to say subsequently, a democratic system has every right to defend itself by curtailing rights and freedoms in the face of political, economic or world crises. "A democratic nation, attacked by an aggressor, has every right to limit democracy if this is found necessary in the interests of national security."[122] In a nutshell, Churchill was right because, although democracy has defects, citizens have "good reason to suspect any system that claims to be perfect, because such claims are usually a mask either for insanity or for evil".[123] Democracy is not an easy system to operate. It often attracts ingratitude from citizens by way of criticism and even abuse, sometimes defended as free speech. But de Cruz concludes with an overwhelming endorsement of the superiority of democracy.

> Democracy is not an angelic system: its virtues do not shine out so overwhelmingly that it can be immediately and easily seen to be totally superior to its competitors. Often it is covered in such shabby, worn and tattered robes that its real virtues are effectively hidden and no one pays it much attention.... [But for] all its deficiencies, democracy is the only system that gives us, the ordinary people, a chance to be human, a chance to live like human beings, a chance to get up from our knees and be the kind of man or woman we would like to be.[124]

De Cruz's article elicited an extraordinarily perceptive rejoinder from Ronnie Quek, a Secondary 3 student of St. Joseph's Institution. He argued that democracy is government based on rule by the people, who are valuable as individuals and who possess inalienable rights that must be preserved and not be removed through deception, propaganda and tyranny. "Your article has given a very poor definition of democracy", the boy exclaimed, because democracy is not limited, constitutional and rotatory. Democracy cannot be altered according to the tastes of leaders just because it exists under human conditions. People should be free to speak the truth freely. "Let us not resort to un-democratic measures to abolish him by arresting and sentencing him into [*sic*] prison without a fair trial or even under the false pretence of security." He continued: "Remember, the laws of the state are passed by the majority, not to protect the majority, but the individual." He concludes with a demand: "Let us then hold free elections, elections in which the election slips do not contain serial numbers."[125]

Replying in the same issue, de Cruz generously welcomed the "splendid re-affirmations of the rights of man and the glories of democracy" in the boy's stimulating letter. He pointed out that, contrary to his young interlocutor's understanding, he had not used the terms "limited", "rotatory" and "constitutional" as limitations on the need for democracy, but in fact as descriptions of how democracy served the people by remaining relevant in changing situations and placing restrictions on government actions. Both Ronnie and he "esteem democracy as a jewel without peer, to be forever esteemed among men". But it was necessary to have rigorous security laws to defend democracy against the Malayan Communist Party's "war on incipient democracy both in Singapore and in Malaysia", even after both states became independent. It was only as a matter of strategy that the MCP was conducting a shooting war on the Thai–Malaysian border. "When it can it will turn its guns, without mercy, on us. Believe me, I know. I was a Communist for many years."[126]

Notes

1. Lee Kuan Yew, *The Singapore Story: Memoirs of Lee Kuan Yew* (Singapore, Times Editions, 1998), p. 321.
2. Ibid.
3. Ibid.
4. "Message from Minister", *Bakti: Journal of the Political Study Centre*, no. 1 (July 1960): 3.
5. OHI, p. 123.
6. OHI, p. 124.
7. OHI, pp. 125–26.
8. Robert Yeo, *Routes: A Singaporean Memoir 1940–75* (Singapore: Ethos Books, 2011), pp. 154–55.
9. Interview with Ann Wee.
10. Interview with former president S.R. Nathan. He says that he was disappointed when he heard that de Cruz had moved to Sarawak. De Cruz had known "all the reasons why we had the friction" with the Malaysian government; indeed, he had been a part of the debate over a Malaysian Malaysia. "I was disappointed when he

shifted to Sarawak to work and live there because somebody who had committed himself to something was suddenly going to do the opposite", Nathan says. "Rahman Ya'kub was not the best of friends with Singapore", he adds. "He was a [Malay] ultra. I could not understand how de Cruz went to Sarawak to work for him." It was a "contradiction" that somebody who was "highly principled, politically active, and knew all the difficulties when we had been a part of Malaysia", and in fact had been witness to them, could go there.

11. OHI, p. 126.
12. N.C. Saxena, *Virtuous Cycles: The Singapore Public Service and National Development* (Singapore: UNDP, Civil Service College and Ministry of Foreign Affairs, 2011), p. 40.
13. "Greek Political Thought", Papers, 173, p. 1.
14. Ibid., p. 3.
15. Ibid., p. 3.
16. Ibid., p. 5.
17. "Ideas of the British Parliamentary Revolution of the 17th Century", Papers, 173, p. 1.
18. Ibid., p. 2.
19. Gerald de Cruz, "John Locke", Papers, 173/028/007, pp. 2–3.
20. Ibid., pp. 6–7.
21. Ibid., p. 3.
22. Gerald de Cruz, "Rousseau and the General Will", Papers, 173/032, p. 1.
23. Ibid., p. 3.
24. Ibid., pp. 4–5.
25. Ibid., p. 8.
26. Ibid., p. 7.
27. Gerald de Cruz, "The American Revolution", Papers, 173/030, p. 2.
28. Ibid., pp. 3–4.
29. Ibid., p. 8.
30. Ibid., p. 10.

31. Ibid., p. 14.
32. Gerald de Cruz, "The French Revolution", Papers, 173/034, pp. 1–3.
33. Gerald de Cruz, "Burke and Conservatism", Papers, 173/037, pp. 1–14.
34. Gerald de Cruz, "A Survey of Communism — *The Communist Manifesto*", Papers, 173, pp. 1–2.
35. Gerald de Cruz, "Lenin's Theory of the Professional Revolutionary", Papers, 173/060, p. 1.
36. Gerald de Cruz, "Communism Old and New", Papers, 32/11, pp. 1–3.
37. Gerald de Cruz, "The Fabian Society", Papers, 154/004, p. 1.
38. Ibid.
39. Ibid.
40. Gerald de Cruz, "The Conflict of Generations", Papers, 57/13, p. 1.
41. Ibid., p. 2.
42. Ibid.
43. Gerald de Cruz, "Transcript of Lecture by Mr. De Cruz on the Young Intellectuals of Singapore", Papers, 179/29, p. 12.
44. Gerald de Cruz, "Need for an Ideology", Papers, 56/7, p. 1.
45. Ibid., p. 2.
46. Gerald de Cruz, *Nationalism* (Singapore: Donald Moore for Asia Pacific Press, 1969).
47. Ibid., p. 2.
48. Ibid., p. 5.
49. Ibid., p. 7.
50. Ibid., p. 9.
51. Ibid., p. 8.
52. Ibid., p. 9.
53. Ibid., p. 10.
54. Ibid., p. 10.
55. Ibid., p. 11.
56. Ibid., p. 12.

57. Ibid., p. 14.
58. Ibid., p. 15.
59. Ibid., p. 18.
60. Ibid., p. 17.
61. Ibid., p. 21.
62. Ibid., p. 23.
63. Ibid., p. 26.
64. Ibid., pp. 34–35.
65. Ibid., p. 37.
66. Gerald de Cruz, *Forum on Nationalism* (Singapore: Donald Moore for Asia Pacific Press, 1969).
67. Ibid., pp. 1–3.
68. Ibid., pp. 26–27.
69. Ibid., p. 6.
70. Ibid., pp. 10–11.
71. Ibid., pp. 5–6.
72. Ibid., p. 7.
73. Ibid., pp. 12–15.
74. Ibid., p. 4.
75. Ibid., p. 10.
76. Ibid., p. 20.
77. Ibid., p. 21.
78. Ibid., p. 21.
79. Ibid., pp. 22–23.
80. Ibid., pp. 25–26.
81. Ibid., p. 29.
82. Ibid., p. 30.
83. Ibid., p. 30.
84. Ibid., p. 31.
85. Ibid., p. 33.
86. Ibid., p. 34.
87. Gerald de Cruz, *Communism* (Singapore: Donald Moore for Asia Pacific Press, 1971).
88. Ibid., pp. 1–2.

89. Ibid., p. 2.
90. Ibid., p. 3.
91. Ibid., p. 3.
92. Ibid., p. 4.
93. Ibid., p. 6.
94. Ibid., p. 16.
95. Ibid., p. 20.
96. Ibid., pp. 20–21.
97. Ibid., pp. 22–23.
98. Ibid., pp. 25–27.
99. Ibid., p. 30.
100. Ibid., p. 34.
101. Ibid., p. 35.
102. Ibid., p. 36.
103. Ibid., p. 38.
104. Ibid., p. 38.
105. Ibid., pp. 38–39.
106. Gerald de Cruz, *Forum on Communism* (Singapore: Donald Moore for Asia Pacific Press, 1971).
107. Ibid., pp. 1–4.
108. Ibid., pp. 6–7.
109. Ibid., pp. 5–6.
110. Ibid., p. 9.
111. Ibid., p. 9.
112. Ibid., p. 15.
113. Ibid., p. 23.
114. Ibid., p. 24.
115. Ibid., p. 26.
116. Ibid., p. 27.
117. Ibid., p. 30.
118. Ibid., pp. 30–41.
119. Ibid., p. 33.
120. Gerald de Cruz, "Your Questions Answered — Democracy", *Prospect*, August 1969.

121. Ibid., pp. 23–24.
122. Ibid., p. 25.
123. Ibid., p. 25.
124. Ibid., p. 25.
125. "Letters from Readers", *Prospect,* December 1969, p. 31.
126. Gerald de Cruz's reply, Ibid., pp. 31–32.

Chapter 9

FRIEND OF LABOUR

Gerald de Cruz's association with the labour movement involved his friendship with C.V. Devan Nair during the MDU years. Nair, who was a teacher at St. Andrew's School, was impressed by P.V. Sharma and became his assistant in the Singapore Teachers' Union. Nair asked de Cruz whether he should go into politics or into the trade union movement. De Cruz suggested that he consider devoting himself full-time to trade unions. But the friendship between the two took off only in the 1970s, when Nair was modernizing the labour movement as chief of the National Trades Union Congress (NTUC). In his work and personal relationships, de Cruz said, Nair was an extremely efficient and inspiring person, a very generous and compassionate man. De Cruz admired his tremendous courage when he finally took a stand and stood beside Lee Kuan Yew against his former comrades like Lim Chin Siong and developed the trade union movement. De Cruz steered clear of this battle, but he came back into the picture when the unions had begun to work in partnership with the government and the management to build a new Singapore. De Cruz, who chaired the NTUC's information and publicity committee, helped with the modernization movement and was awarded a gold medal by the NTUC in 1970 for his efforts as a friend of labour. Later, he became the assistant editor of *Perjuangan*, the monthly journal of the NTUC, which he actually edited because the official editor was not a journalist. He also helped to edit the periodicals of the Singapore Industrial Labour Organization (SILO), the Pioneer Industries Employees' Union (PIEU), and the Consumer Association of Singapore (CASE).[1]

However, it was not only his journalistic skills that de Cruz brought with him to his work for the NTUC. His political instincts, honed during both his communist years and during his time at the Political Study Centre, enabled him to view labour issues in the light of broader social interests.

This is seen in his contribution to the NTUC's Seminar on the Modernization of the Labour Movement, held in November 1969. The times were dire. The British had announced in 1968 that they would withdraw their military forces from Singapore. This would not only lead to direct unemployment for those working in the British bases, but would also hurt the wider economy badly because British military spending accounted for a significant part of Singapore's gross domestic product. In the NTUC's own account of its role in those difficult times, it recalls how the labour movement supported both moves to transform the bases for civilian use and the stimulation of the economy by inviting in foreign investors in a big way. "Laws were enacted to clearly delineate functions of management and those of trade unions. While union leaders understood the rationale for the legislation, they were upset because it reduced their scope for negotiations", the NTUC said. "Nevertheless, they endorsed the Employment Act after being assured by the government that employers would not be allowed to ride roughshod over workers. [The] NTUC's support for the new law led to a massive inflow of investments." All the same, changes on the labour scene "had an unsettling effect on workers in the unionised sector. Morale dipped. Membership dropped to low levels." To turn the tide, the NTUC organized the modernization seminar. "We opted for cooperation instead of confrontation in dealings with management."[2]

De Cruz's paper on workers' education presented at the seminar addresses labour in the specific context of Singapore. It calls for ways in which the labour movement can "play a full role in equal working partnership with the Government and management" to achieve a satisfactory standard of living for all citizens within a democratic framework. Indeed, a democratic society is the best guarantee of workers' liberties, while a strong labour movement in turn is one of the bastions of democracy. Workers need to support "the twin pillars of government planning and free economic competition". The objects are full and "permanent employment suited to the needs and abilities of workers" in an environment where wealth and incomes are distributed justly and equitably and the abuse of economic power will be eliminated. To this end, workers' education should enable unionists to think freely and independently about problems involving the labour movement.[3] On that front, there are "many dimensions in our situation that were unknown in the West at a similar stage of development of their trade unions". Singapore was undergoing at least four revolutions telescoped into one: a political, an economic, a social and a cultural revolution. In addition, "our economic revolution itself is four-revolutions-in-one — machine, mass production, computer and electronic — all intermeshed in our grim struggle for survival". On the global front, the pendulum of power had swung from the Atlantic to the Pacific, and the old great powers of France, Holland and Britain had given way to the United States, the Soviet Union and China. In the circumstances, a trade unionist would have to understand "the new dimensions in pattern and power in which he lives and works". He would have to possess a sophisticated awareness of the forces reshaping world history. Hence, courses in areas such as the "changes and contradictions" of international communism, the reshaping of the Southeast Asian power structure, and the dynamics of nation-building in Singapore needed to be as much a part of the new trade union education as courses in trade union structure or collective bargaining.[4]

De Cruz's paper goes on to discuss various methods that could be used in workers' education. The lecture is suitable for one-way communication in getting across information and views, but its drawback is that it often attracts few questions and so falls short on audience participation. Hence it might be a good idea to begin a conference with a short lecture and move on to breaking up into groups for discussion. Or there could just be a discussion, which is a two-way form of communication. It stimulates group involvement by giving everyone a chance to be heard. "The lecture is an authoritarian medium whereas the discussion is a democratic one", he argues. "To absorb information, to understand the drift of ideas, to exchange information and experience, to analyse facts and opinions, to correct misinformation and to modify or change attitudes, no technique is more effective than the discussion technique. It is also capable of anticipating problems, relieving tensions, and stimulating action."[5] The discussion method has its disadvantages: It can become boring or be dominated by an aggressive participant, thereby creating tension. But a good discussion leader could prevent or reduce these problems, and audio-visual techniques could keep participants engaged. The small group discussion, consisting of four to seven members a group, is another useful technique. It could address a specific problem, or each group could tackle a different aspect of the subject under study. Each group secretary would report its opinions to the whole class for comment or criticism, and an overall reporter would summarize the entire proceedings. Then there were workshops that allowed participants to work together on common projects, in the course of which they could attend lectures, take part in discussion or sub-discussion groups, go on field tours, or work on practical projects.[6]

Making specific recommendations, the paper calls for the NTUC and its affiliated unions to establish a Workers' College along the lines of the central institute which community centres have for the training of youth leaders. Full-time officers responsible only for trade-union education should be employed, both at the NTUC level and at the union level. There should be at least one full-time education officer in every union.[7]

De Cruz's deep human interest in the worker — who meant far more to him than labour, a mere factor of production along with land and capital — shines through powerfully in his erudite contribution to the NTUC symposium, "Labour in a Technological Society: Action Programme for the 70's", held in April 1973. In a paper entitled "The Dynamics of Motivation and Productivity", he begins with a scathing dismissal of management theorists such as Frederick Taylor, whose theory of scientific management saw management through the lens of industrial engineering. De Cruz notes that it was "this type of industrial society which Charlie Chaplin satirised so effectively in his film, Modern Times". He rejects notions of both the "physical worker" — the man whom material comforts made productive — and the "emotional worker", "who sought direction, not from the rational and logical directives of management, but from his own deep emotional needs, and his irrational colleagues".[8]

The latter notion was a management response to the work of a Harvard Graduate School of Business Administration team led by Elton Mayo, which carried out its research at the Hawthorne works of the Western Electric Company in Chicago between

1927 and 1932. Mayo's findings were confirmed by another study carried out by Abraham Zaleznik and his co-workers at the Harvard Business School. The study found that, except possibly for employment itself, rewards offered by management meant far less to workers than membership of a group. "Group Formation was a reaction to the frozen environment of the job which was created by management's attitude that the workers would not be much more competent when they retired than when they were hired", de Cruz writes. "In distinct contrast, group membership gave workers a sense of belonging, defined their status and presented them with a human way of life."[9]

De Cruz moves on to a study of Rensis Likert's and Daniel Katz's 1947 research on the behaviour and attitudes of first-line supervisors. They identified two types of supervisor — the "production-centred" one and the "employee-centred" one — and showed conclusively that the latter led highly productive groups. Consequently, changes in management philosophy saw the concept of the push-button worker being replaced among enlightened managers with the recognition that the worker, like every other person, has complex and shifting needs. Also, humanistic and democratic values began to take precedence over depersonalized, mechanistic and bureaucratic organizational ideas. In 1959, three behavioural scientists, F. Herzberg, M. Mausner and B. Snyderman, launched several studies which identified two distinct attitudes of workers to their jobs. One emanated from "dissatisfiers", factors that made for job dissatisfaction, and the other reflected "motivators", factors that made for job motivation. The major job dissatisfiers were company policy and administration, supervision, salary, interpersonal relations, and working conditions. The major job motivators were the job itself, responsibility, achievement, advancement, and recognition. De Cruz points out that the dissatisfiers all relate to the worker's environment, while the motivators define his relationship to the job. "Both set of factors are necessary for mental equilibrium but only the personal growth factors develop genuine and durable motivation", he comments.[10]

This particular study dealt with engineers and accountants in Pittsburgh. Subsequent studies carried out by others extended the scope to supervisors, women civil servants, administrators, managerial employees, scientists, male technicians, female hourly assemblers, nurses, unskilled workers, housekeeping hospital workers, Air Force officers, and manufacturing employees — a broad swathe of the labour landscape. The new studies confirmed the results of the first one. Newer studies spread across the political landscape, from Finland to Hungary and the Soviet Union itself, where there were disturbing problems of absenteeism, low morale, alcoholism and moonlighting. Researchers at the University of Leningrad found that "the highest relationship was with the nature of the work; the next highest was between the worker and his job, while the lowest relationship was with the social value of the job".[11] De Cruz comments perceptively: "Irrespective of ideology and other fundamental differences between the capitalist and the communist system, and despite the conflicting claims of each to serve man more fully than the other, the workers in both systems demand the same thing: that their job, its nature and its organisation should be such as to give them a sense of worth, of achievement and the promise of advancement."[12] De Cruz cites Herzberg's formulation that workers, like other men, have two interdependent but independent sides to their nature. The Adam side reflects the primordial need to find food, drink and shelter. The Abraham side demands that work, which occupies nearly half of a man's life, should recognize the worker's humanity. Of course, de Cruz adds, productivity must appeal to both sides of human nature. Satisfying the worker's material needs is necessary because he cannot function without them, but doing so is not sufficient because satisfaction is both temporary and not really a motivation. "Motivation can only come from the worker himself, and he will produce more results only when his job pushes him to do so by feeding his Abraham needs."[13]

However, with an eye clearly on the Singapore context, de Cruz serves a reminder that wages are important. The studies cited in his paper were all carried out in the developed world, where wages were considerably higher than in the Third World. "Where, in an under-developed country, the opportunity to increase one's status, or power, or sense of achievement is still a long way away, then money is seen as the only way to improve standards of living, and workers will seek to maximise their wages. Fair wages must be paid and they must be seen by the worker to be fair."[14] Where trade unions come into the picture is that they have been the main instruments through which workers have developed a sense of self-worth in spite of the exploitative tendencies of employers. Labour solidarity has been shaped by conflict between unions and the management. Singapore is different. "Here it is the trade unions which have taken the initiative to change the climate of industrial relations in order to increase motivation and enhance productivity", de Cruz remarks.[15] The unspoken but natural quid pro quo of his words is that the climate of industrial peace underwritten by trade unions can last only so long as employers keep their side of the bargain.

De Cruz ends his paper with several recommendations. He calls on the NTUC to urge all firms to restructure their Industrial Relations division into two divisions. One division would deal with salaries, working conditions and so on. As usual, the Personnel Department would represent the management in this division. The other division would be the Department of Motivation that would deal with both workers and the management. It would restructure jobs so as to give workers a sense of accomplishment and recognize his contributions. The worker should understand more about his job than he does now, take greater responsibility for doing it, and should be able to move to higher levels of achievement. The Department of Motivation would move into three areas of remedial work — technological obsolescence, poor performance, and administrative failure — and find solutions to these problems. The department would also review corporate assumptions, practices, rules and policies to engage in discarding those that had become irrelevant. Trade union representatives must sit in on the department's deliberations so that workers accept it on its merits. Indeed, this representation would constitute a part of workers' responsibility for job performance. Singapore trade unionists should be sent on visits to companies in the United States, which have such departments, to see how their experiences could be translated into industrial relations in Singapore. The NTUC should also urge the National Productivity Board and employers' federations to study the dynamics of motivation and send their representatives to study the American practice of the new industrial psychology with the objective of adapting it to the Singapore environment.[16]

A study of labour protection and social insurance, along with workers' productivity, took de Cruz, not to the United States, but to the Soviet Union in 1970. Along with unionist V.R. Balakrishnan, he represented the NTUC at the May Day celebrations in Moscow. Over the following ten days, their Russian trade union hosts did their best to tell them how the Soviet Union protected its workers. They were briefed on the main issues by Anatoly Semonov, chief of the Department of Labour Protection of the All-Union Council of Trade Unions.

De Cruz came away from Moscow with a definite view: "There is, perhaps, no more extensive scheme of labour protection for workers in the world than is found in the Soviet Union today. It has many important ingredients which are worth our earnest consideration in Singapore."[17] Semonov defined labour protection as the solving of technical, organizational, hygienic and legal problems so as to ensure safe and healthy working conditions. This involved establishing the norms and rules regulating conditions of work, with special rules applying to young people and women and those working under dangerous conditions. In the Soviet Union, no law could be adopted on these two categories without the consent of trade unions. The safety measures were included in the contract between the management and labour, and the funds for implementing these clauses in the contract, which amounted to more than 1,000 billion roubles in 1969, came from the enterprise itself. Also, over the preceding fifty years, enterprises had taken part in a special competition for better labour protection. In 1969, more than ninety per cent of enterprises had taken part in the national contest, which showcased how workers themselves could organize effective schemes of industrial hygiene.[18]

Soviet trade unions employed more than 4,000 qualified technical inspectors who had the right to demand that safety rules be observed and that proposals for improvement be implemented. No enterprise, shop or unit could begin production without the permission of the inspectors, whose powers ranged from imposing fines and reporting the administration to the trade union council concerned to asking for the dismissal of the manager and bringing a complaint before special judicial tribunals. The inspectors were assisted by two and a half million volunteers drawn from the ranks of workers, who were usually the best workers in the plant, had been elected by trade unionists and had been trained for this particular job. The volunteers had the right to enter any enterprise at any time of the day or night and exercise control over safety measures. They ensured that the special regulations for youth — no overtime, no night work, no heavy jobs, and holidays in summer — were followed, as were those for pregnant workers: no work at night, and two months' full leave with pay before and after childbirth.[19]

Every trade union organized its own labour protection committee at the place of work. Consisting of the voluntary social workers, trade union representatives, and the technical inspector, the committee reported periodically to the trade union committee of the enterprise concerned. It organized special training for the social workers, and invited the chief engineer or manager to attend its meetings, particularly if important complaints were going to be made. When conflicts arose with the management, the trade union could take up the matter to the city, territorial and, finally, all-Union levels.

Soviet labour unions enjoyed impressive research backup. In addition to the more than a hundred state-run institutes of scientific research into labour protection, the All-Union Council of Trade Unions itself ran six such institutes. The Moscow Institute, which de Cruz visited, dealt with issues such as improving ventilation systems for toxic gases, industrial acoustics, and the analysis of industrial injuries. The institute in Leningrad studied the effects of industrial noise; the one in Tbilisi the special problems of the mining industry; in Sverdlovsk the physiology and psychology of workers; in Ivanov the special problems of women workers; and in Kagan, the dangers of high humidity.

De Cruz recalls the "eloquent and persuasive" Semonov as saying: "Don't forget. The secret in labour protection is norms. Establish your norms and the rest will follow." De Cruz's conclusion: "I think it is very good advice to Singapore trade unions."[20]

Veteran unionist and former Minister of State Yu-Foo Yee Shoon, who first met de Cruz in the early 1970s, sums up his contribution to the labour movement. "In the past, SILO had comprised mostly Chinese-educated unionists and staff; the English-educated staff had Cambridge O-Level qualifications. De Cruz was an English-educated intellectual." Recalling how he assisted the union in its English media relations and publications, she adds that his work went beyond that. "During our general meetings and membership recruitment, he would brief workers on the benefits of joining the union and discuss collective bargaining. I was often asked to be his interpreter because many of the staff could speak only Mandarin. Working with him helped improve my public speaking and oratory skills. He taught me how to present my ideas in a simple and concise manner which could get across to workers easily." What helped in reaching out to the masses was de Cruz's demeanour. He dressed "humbly" and had a smile. "He was amicable and approachable. The workers would warm up to him quickly. They never felt uncomfortable with him. He was an understanding and patient teacher. His fatherly demeanour made him well-liked and respected." Commenting on his legacy, she says: "Young Singaporeans can learn from him to be more socially-conscious of the lower-income group."[21]

Notes

1. OHI, pp. 248–51. In a letter dated 4 January 2006 to Janadas Devan, son of C.V. Devan Nair, offering condolences on the death of the trade union leader, Gerald de Cruz's daughter Judith Prakash wrote: "My father was also active in the SILO-PIEU unions whence it was that he worked closely with Phey Yew Kok. My father expressed certain misgivings on Phey's character to your father. Your father trusted Phey implicitly at that time and could not believe what he was told. Relations cooled a little between our fathers but not to the point of breach." Indeed, as President of Singapore, Devan Nair heard of de Cruz, who was in Sarawak, having suffered strokes and

needing treatment for his eyes. "Without hesitation (and indeed unknown to me) he arranged for funding through Rotary and got my father flown to Singapore. Arthur Lim was the doctor. Arthur waived his fees", Judith Prakash added in the letter. "Your father attended every day at the Mt. Elizabeth Hospital for a few hours to keep my father company. During those visits, he used to recite poetry to my father and, in particular, recite and act 'Shakuntala' by Aurobindo. Towards the end of the stay, your father called me and asked if he could take my father and stepmother to Istana Villa to stay with him for a few days. I was more than happy to agree although I am not sure that I could have said no."

2. <http://www.ntuc.org.sg/wps/portal/up2/home/aboutntuc/organisationprofile/aboutus/historyofntuc/historyofntuc details?WCM_GLOBAL_CONTEXT=/content_library/ntuc/home/about+ntuc/organisation+profile/about+us/history+of+ntuc/e2169800450fb13ab882fe96656b86bc>.
3. Gerald de Cruz, "Education for Leadership in the Labour Movement", in *Why Labour Must Go Modern: The NTUC Case for a Modernized Labour Movement* (Singapore: National Trades Union Congress, 1970), pp. 152–54.
4. Ibid., pp. 158–59.
5. Ibid., p. 157.
6. Ibid., pp. 157–58.
7. Ibid., p. 155.
8. Gerald de Cruz, "The Dynamics of Motivation and Productivity", Workshop III, Proceedings, NTUC Symposium, "Labour in a Technological Society: Action Programme for the 70's", April 1973, pp. 1–2.
9. Ibid., p. 2.
10. Ibid., p. 4.
11. Ibid., p. 5.
12. Ibid., p. 5.
13. Ibid., p. 7.
14. Ibid., pp. 7–8.

15. Ibid., p. 8.
16. Ibid., pp. 8–10.
17. Gerald de Cruz, "Industrial Health in the Soviet Union", *Perjuangan,* June 1970, p. 8.
18. Ibid.
19. Ibid.
20. Ibid.
21. Interview with Yu-Foo Yee Shoon.

Chapter 10

THE COLUMNIST

Between 1971 and 1974, de Cruz was a columnist for the *New Nation*, of which he was also Diplomatic Editor. His columns and occasional editorials, whether on international or domestic affairs, are marked by a combative humanism that takes on a range of issues from communism and race to sex and juvenile delinquency. Invariably trenchant, often wry and irreverent, sometimes controversial, occasionally contentious and at times spoiling for an intellectual fight, his writings revel in the columnist's art — to provoke the reader to some purpose. His favourite enemies are ignorance and hypocrisy in society. Cant and humbug passing off for tradition and orthodoxy are a standing invitation to his jousting rejoinders, while pompous piety over matters of sex and religion arouses his cynical indignation and attracts sharp, withering rebuttals. His style is convivial and occasionally anecdotal — the aromatic air of a coffee shop conversation lingers deliciously over it — but there is a clear conclusion which reflects long and clear thinking presented logically and impassioned by the courage of conviction.

His columns dismiss the ideological claims of both Bolshevism and Chinese communism. In a defence of the ideological legitimacy of revisionism, which communists revile, he compares them with "all good 'Bible-thumping' fundamentalists" who have "an extraordinary litany of abuse for heresies and heretics". Recalling the revisionism of the socialist Eduard Bernstein, de Cruz supports his critical approach to Marxism. Bernstein "heavily decried the Utopian element in communism — all the guff about heaven on earth being realised eventually under the communist system, when the state would wither away, and, as Lenin said, every cook could become Prime Minister and every Prime Minister could cook".[1] However, de Cruz's break with communism did not blind him to the opportunities being created in Asia by fundamental shifts such as the Sino–American rapprochement of the early 1970s, the Vietnam War, and consequently the prospects of the Association of Southeast Asian Nations (ASEAN). He took a keen interest in geopolitical and diplomatic trends that would influence the fortunes of Singapore.

Thus, he sounds a discordant note in the midst of the general rejoicing over China having lifted the bamboo curtain to admit table-tennis players and journalists from America. "One of the great virtues of China's isolation has been that it became the focus of hope[s] and dreams for all those who, for one reason or another, appeared to have lost hope for, or in, the rest of the world", he writes in a 1971 column. Utopia has gripped the human imagination to the extent that it has to be invented, as Plato, Thomas More and St. Augustine did, or constructed, as people have sought to do from time to time. "In modern times the search for Utopia has usually been conducted within the framework of Communism, because no other ideology has dared to promise more and no other religion has had quite the impertinence to locate its heaven on earth, as Communism does." In a ringing denunciation of the violence and oppression that lay beneath the surface of the utopianism of the Soviet Union, he says:

> For a generation it was Stalinism that meant Utopia for many all over the world. The rivers of blood shed inside the Soviet Union were converted into torrents of hosannas, once they crossed the border, by the news media which were totally controlled by the Stalinists; and, with the willing connivance of the communist leaders of the world, a picture was built up of a new man in Soviet society, indeed of a new society, in which the old millstones round our necks had been forever crushed, and in which we had been able to take the great leap forward from the kingdom of necessity into the kingdom of freedom.

That murderous myth did not outlast the departure of Stalin. Now, with the walls of Chinese isolation falling to "the incongruous waving of ping-pong bats", the Chinese utopia might not survive scrutiny, as its Soviet predecessor had not.[2]

This critically realist approach to communism in China is balanced, nevertheless, by a profound sense of the changes sweeping the country. In a moving commentary, he describes how rural communes enabled Chinese peasants to fight back at long last against locusts that had devastated crops. Two things mattered in this struggle: organization, and numbers. The communes organized people in their millions to fight against a dreaded natural calamity. But the Chinese could be organized on this scale only because they possessed the numbers in the first place. This observation leads de Cruz to argue, first, that the Chinese peasants who ate many of the locusts would not be content with their fate forever; second, that when China's economic development took off, it would be faced with the same challenge of extending its control over the world's resources and markets that had confronted the Americans; and, third, that economic development would lead to military expansion, as with the Japanese. Maoist China might abjure mass consumption and choose to remain voluntarily at an intermediate stage of development, but such self and collective discipline was unlikely to survive Mao.[3]

How prescient de Cruz was on every front has been proved by the more than three decades of China's development. China is Asia's leading economic power and positioned for a global role. Consumption is a marked feature of its domestic economic life. Its neighbours and others worry that its assertiveness on the regional and world stage reflects its burgeoning military confidence. Although de Cruz did not go so far as to posit a Chinese threat, he visualized a trajectory combining economic and military change that is evident in many aspects of China's rise. His close reading of history and of the political classics, his deep participation in the inner life of the communist movement, and his attention to the nuances of development and change in international relations equipped him with the tools to describe and analyse events with an eye on their long-term implications. This is the primary reason why his journalistic writings, like his theoretical excursions into political thought, possess a freshness found lacking in commentaries of the time devoted to the minutiae of micro-developments and incremental change.

Another sense in which de Cruz had an eye on the future was his understanding of what is called globalization today. In a column, he professes the belief that the "sharp distinction between domestic and foreign policies that has been a feature of sovereign, territorially-based nation states will be removed, and in its place there will be growing pressures for common policies and procedures by which countries discuss and co-ordinate actions that until now have been regarded as of domestic concern exclusively". Citing the work of the Yale economist Richard Cooper, he asks his readers to contemplate the emergence of a new world economic order in which the logic of growing interdependence will overtake economic interaction based on national boundaries and policies.[4]

It is in that evolving context, and in spite of his reservations about both Chinese and American foreign policy approaches, that de Cruz welcomed the Sino-American rapprochement of the early 1970s. He writes that "it would be downright foolish for President Nixon to delay his trip to Peking too long, allowing fate or the powerful opponents of an American detente with China the opportunity to sabotage his peace-making trip". Recalling the assassinations of President John Kennedy, his brother Robert Kennedy and the black American leader Martin Luther King, de Cruz points out that these three victims "were believed to have the power, as Nixon has today, to make a radical change in the policies of the American government" and it is "this possibility that arouses hysteria among the various paranoid strains in American political life".[5] De Cruz is capable as well of demonstrating a deeply felt humanism, as when he reiterates the need for a political solution in Vietnam:

> An entire generation of Vietnamese has been born, grown up, and entered manhood and womanhood, which does not know peace.... Many have lost even the ability to cry. Wounded, maimed, with hands or legs shot off, even children scarcely whimper. Their eyes are dry.... People, it is true, are resilient; cultures can take enormous stress. But the Vietnamese people and culture are, some consider, dissolving under the weight of the interminable war, and its devastating infrastructure of displacement, distortion and dehumanisation.[6]

On the domestic scene, race attracts de Cruz's vehement denunciation. He argues that common beliefs about race are "so empty of meaning and so full of prejudice" that even the use of the term is dangerous. He dismisses the idea that certain fixed and unchangeable physical, intellectual and psychological characteristics are handed down from one generation, distinguishing Chinese, Malays and Indians from one another. The truth is that, even among the three major human classifications — the Caucasian, the Negroid and the Mongoloid — differences within these groups are as wide as the differences among them. No group enjoys any exclusive set of characteristics; instead, these overlap among groups. "Race is a myth, and a dangerous one. When the leader of one particular ethnic group shouts out to his compatriots, 'we are of the same blood,' he should go and tell it to the blood transfusion service!"[7] (De Cruz, as noted earlier, was a serial blood donor: He began at the age of 30 and by 62 he had donated 62 pints over 62 sessions!)[8] He concludes adamantly: "There is no Chinese race, or Indian race, or Malay race, or European race, or black race, or white race, or yellow race. There is only one race to which we all belong, the human race."[9] In the following week's column, he highlights the importance of custom and culture over that of race, observing with wry triumphalism that a Chinese Muslim would "retreat as energetically" from a pig as "a non-Muslim Chinese will advance towards it" with "visions of roast pork crackling" in his imagination. "It is culture which interprets a fact for us and makes us recognise it, or blinds us to it, or impels us to trample on it." But even culture is a man-made artefact. It is the response of humans to their environment, the body of learned experience transmitted down by fathers and grandfathers (and foremothers, de Cruz might have added) "as they struggled with life and tried to bring it under control". Consequently, there are no superior and inferior cultures, only different cultures. He shows that the Australian aborigine's understanding of marriage is "so subtle, exhaustive and detailed" that some sociologists hail "these first Australians as the fathers of the science of social measurement in the social sciences". Many so-called primitive cultures "put many so-called modern societies to shame". Turning to Singapore, he warns that it is culture and not race that divides people. "For race is a myth and myths are notoriously difficult to dislodge. But culture is man-made, and therefore can be modified and changed." Thus, it is possible for Singapore to enjoy a national culture that is "varied but coherent".[10]

In the same vein of progressive and open-minded thinking, he implores educationists to find out what the values of young Singaporeans are, because, otherwise, the result will be to present the values, biases and prejudices of older generations. He laments the fact that *Woodstock* had been banned from the screens, but that the television series, *Combat,* which glorifies "war, sadism and deviations from the truth", is permitted to be screened. Likewise, the film, *Stiletto,* was withdrawn because it showed a woman's bare breast for a fraction of a second; however, it is possible to see actual bare breasts and more at nightclubs if one has the money. Young people who find these contradictions hypocritical "are not rebellious or subversive — they are simply observant and intelligent". "They draw the logical conclusions — but since ours is the kind of young, struggling society in which open protest is not received kindly, they suppress their criticism, and then they are jeered at for being apathetic."[11]

Some of his columns reveal tender empathy with what makes humans vulnerable and rise to gentle compassion for fragile and fallible man. Pointing out that the traumas which a baby may experience at and after birth can affect him deeply for the rest of his life, he writes movingly of the mother's irreplaceable role in the life of the infant. "It is her arms which enfold it, her breast which feeds it, her caress which makes it feel that it has a rightful place in the world, that it is loved and wanted, and that it is needed." All babies can tolerate the absence of their mothers up to a point, but beyond it, separation-anxiety can result in hysteria, depression and dread. Left unattended, panic attacks develop into neuroses in later life: compulsive detachment from others, fixations or phobias. Obsessive attention-seeking or excessive self-effacement; a domineering personality that seeks to compel others to do its bidding, or inordinate meekness that seeks safety in emasculated sycophancy towards the powerful; extreme cynicism that treats all human relationships as a fraud, or indefatigable idealism that finds a home in nothing but exaggeration — these are some of the contradictory ways in which the rejected child tries to come to terms with life in later years. The most extreme expression of neurotic behaviour, of a permanent defect or deviation in character stemming from rejection, is suicide. It is the final cry of despair in response to some event that triggers deeply-embedded feelings of loss or defeat repressed since babyhood, that is, in the first two and a half years of a child's life and particularly in the first year.[12]

In another column on children, he comes down hard on a school director who caned an entire class because he could not find out which child had drawn a chalk line on one boy's desk and another on a schoolbag. According to de Cruz, "the children deserved a medal for not sneaking on one of their number, not a collective hiding". He went so far as to compare the act with what the fascists used to do — "shoot down all the men in a village in which one of their soldiers had been killed if they could not find the culprit". Singapore was trying to build a rugged but not a ruthless society which would be a gracious one as well. To the innocent children, the collective punishment would have seemed "brutal and sadistic", he said without mincing words.[13]

The importance of robust social values is central to de Cruz's thinking. In a column, he takes aim at the counter-culture of the West, which stemmed from "a loss of faith in ideology and in politics". It is not that de Cruz was hostile to the West in general or the United States in particular. Not only was he a humanist — who by definition must be a globalist as well — but also, late in 1966, the Singapore Government had sent him to undertake a non-graduating post-graduate course in Politics and Government at George Washington University in Washington DC, under the tutorship of the American foreign policy expert Harold Hinton. Yet, de Cruz displays consistently in his columns an intense distaste for the easy escapism that defined Western counter-culture of the time and which was seeping into a Third World saturated and dazzled by American media products. He was aghast at what he found rampant on American campuses: "a tremendous cynicism in the ability of men to change things for the better by pooling the common effort". But it is with sadness more than anger that de Cruz seeks to understand what is happening in the West. Citing the celebrated American psychologist Bruno Bettelheim's terse comment that no one can be secure in an insecure world, de Cruz looks at the ideological desolation around him and declares: "Young people in the West refuse to carry on a dialogue with life because they find no meaning in it. It's absurd. There is nothing, they feel, which deserves commitment, so they abandon loyalty and belief, and feel glory in rootlessness.... A generation that is asking why confronts and rejects the business mind which asks how."

Asia's simultaneous revolutions — political, economic and cultural — and its commitment to change things for the better act as a buffer between Western alienation and indigenous society. "I think that as long as life has meaning and purpose to it we shall be able to resist the counter-culture of the West, despite its insidious appeal on many fronts." However, he warns against the erosion of values weakening Asian countries. He gives a telling example. While passing a little church in Singapore, he saw a girl dressed in "fetching and provocative hot-pants emerging from

Mass". It was the very church in which his cousin Gloria, when she was ten years old, was prevented from partaking of Holy Communion because "her sleeves did not quite reach her elbows". "Until 10 years ago, even prostitutes would have been too ashamed to wear, in public, the kind of mini-skirt or hot-pants outfit in which every girl parades so proudly today — and in which they can even go to church." He relates a hilarious incident in which the Senior Cambridge class, of one of the premier girls' schools, went on a school excursion to Singapore Harbour. As the boat went round the harbour, the two nuns who were supervising the students nodded approvingly as "youthful girlish voices rang out in a cheery modern song". "It's a good thing for the nuns' peace of mind that they could not distinguish the words of the song which celebrated the varied sexual exploits of its sexually ambivalent hero."[14]

At the same time, however, de Cruz berates with relentless humour those whose sexual conservatism goes against what he considers natural and thus worth celebrating. He derides the views of the well-known medical practitioner Gwee Ah Leng, who suggested that sex without parenthood was wrong and that, in the event one did not want children immediately, self-control was the best form of birth control. "I don't know what kind of a world the good doctor lives in but in my world, when you put two young, healthy, loving, married people in bed together, then what is unnatural, 'not quite right', dreadfully wrong, is for them to keep their hands off each other." As for contraceptives being immoral, he tells the story of a van-driver who earns $120 a month and his wife, a cook who gets $100 a month. "She is only 40 years old but she was married at 14 and she now has 16 children because her husband, though he doesn't know it, is one of the good doctor's most ardent disciples." De Cruz recalls how the good doctor, speaking to pre-university students at Beatty

School, permitted himself to declare that the human species might go out of circulation like the dinosaurs if birth control were to be practised widely. "Who said that there are no more dinosaurs?" de Cruz enquires with exquisite irony. "I think there still are a few around, only they are sometimes rather difficult to identify because they are camouflaged by medical degrees."[15]

Intellectual and polemical combativeness, verbal argumentativeness, the crushing use of irony, or the deadly deployment of satire — these qualities, honed into an art, contribute to the lasting impression left by Gerald de Cruz the columnist. But they are balanced by an equally powerful tenderness at the sight of stricken man, and an even more overwhelming sense of hope that man is greater than the sum of his misfortunes. Thus, de Cruz speaks of Vietnam as a moral force: "You cannot drop the equivalent of one Hiroshima every six days on a poor if courageous people, without its echo reverberating in sensitive human hearts, and even in those which belong to the apparently unfeeling." He sees the war as demonstrating in its own tortured way "mankind's unbreakable solidarity" played out against the conflict between superpower "might" and small-power "tenacity", between "Western megapolis and eastern countryside", and between "modern technology and semi-literate men sealed together by napalm". Much like Virgil in the Fourth Eclogue, he looks ahead to a new age organized by seers, poets and storytellers who can lead man out of a world poisoned by conflict between brothers and the war on nature. New myths are needed to give man fresh powers to act as building blocks of a common universe, to show him that his powers to destroy are matched by his powers to create, and to reveal how "for the first time utopia is possible for all mankind".[16]

But this utopia must be built on the back of human labour and imagination, which can never cease. Work is not only its own reward but is the basic condition of man. Hence the absence of any elegiac tiredness in de Cruz's writings. They give him an earned place in the overlapping lives of his fellow citizens and others. The written word is what he uses to build new realities. Movingly, he tells the story of two workers at a construction site engaged in chiselling stones. When the first is asked what he is doing, he answers matter-of-factly that he is chiselling a stone. The second, who is equally matter-of-fact, says that he is building a cathedral.[17] De Cruz's preference for looking at life through the eyes of the second worker is obvious. The effort to build something bigger than what the raw material of life offers makes him an incorrigible optimist whose faith is often challenged but never defeated. He takes heart from the story of how mankind has succeeded in freeing itself from the shackles of the past to move forward together "along the new global road that now stretches out before us — with all its promises and all its perils.... What men need and demand today is more information about the global journey and the terrain through which it is going to pass". He concludes evocatively: "If you listen carefully you will hear something like a hush everywhere in the world. It's like the hush that comes at the end of winter, just before the first spring flowers break through.... to bring their message of the arrival of a new world."[18]

Ever since he had taken the political highway to the future, it was the lure of a new world that had kept him going. His ripening years only made the journey more urgent.

Notes

1. Gerald de Cruz, "Revisionism an Honourable and Well-tested Path of Social Democracy", *New Nation*, 25 January 1972.
2. "A Small Discordant Note as China Ping Pongs its Way out of Isolation", *New Nation*, 27 April 1971.

3. "People Who Eat Locusts Today Will Not Be Content with Them Forever", *New Nation*, 24 August 1971.
4. "Nationalism Has Haunted the World Too Long and May Be on Way Out", *New Nation*, 11 April 1972.
5. "Any Delay in Nixon's Trip to Peking Will Increase Possibility of Sabotage", *New Nation*, 27 July 1971.
6. "Will the Vietnam War Go on Forever If It Cannot Be 'Vietnamised'?", *New Nation*, 5 April 1971.
7. "The Myth of Race: Common Belief So Empty of Meaning", *New Nation*, 19 January 1971.
8. "At 62 He Has Donated 62 Pints of blood", *Borneo Post*, 11 May 1982.
9. Gerald de Cruz, "The Myth of Race: Common Belief So Empty of Meaning", *New Nation*, 19 January 1971.
10. "When a Fact Is No More Merely a Fact and 'Race' Is a Myth", *New Nation*, 26 January 1971.
11. "Find Out What the Values of Our Young Are as Well!", *New Nation*, 16 February 1971.
12. "Laying the Time-bombs for a Future of Neurosis and Possible Suicide", *New Nation*, 15 June 1971.
13. "A School Principal Has His Problems but Using the Cane Doesn't Solve Them", *New Nation*, 4 April 1972.
14. "Youth in the West Has Lost Its Faith in the Traditional Father Figures", *New Nation*, 23 November 1971.
15. "All About Love, Sex and the Gwee-man", *New Nation*, 23 February 1971.
16. "Vietnam, in Its Own Way, Has Exemplified Man's Unbreakable Solidarity", *New Nation*, 10 November 1972.
17. "Both Did the Same Thing: One Shaped a Stone, the Other Built a Cathedral", *New Nation*, 20 February 1973.
18. "A New World is in the Making", *New Nation*, 28 May 1974.

Chapter 11

THE FAMILY MAN

Gerald de Cruz remains a larger-than-life figure to his three children by two marriages, to Coral in 1949 and to Maimunah in 1970 after Coral had died in 1965.[1]

His eldest child, Judith Prakash, was born in 1951. She remembers him as a loving and warm father who knew how to engage children, tell them stories, and hold them spellbound. He was very welcoming of her friends, treating them as equals and talking to them without condescension. "He always respected them and talked to them as if they would have something interesting to tell him. I was very close to him because he was very communicative. Yes, he had a temper but, on the whole, he made life fun", the Singapore Supreme Court Judge says. He also had a sense of adventure. She remembers travelling with him down Siglap Hill in his Morris Minor, with the roof down and her standing up. Once, a bee got between his glasses and his eye, causing him to lose control and the car to tilt to one side dangerously. Luckily, no one was hurt.

She remembers her father's kind-heartedness, from giving people a lift in his car to bringing home waifs, like a boy who had got into trouble with the law whom he tried to reform. She remembers as well the close relationship that her parents enjoyed. "He was rather patriarchal when it came to being useless at house work, and he was more of the decision-maker than my mother was", she recalls with a smile. "But there were no intellectual differences between my parents. My father believed that women and men were equal. He had no hierarchy in him, no sense of being better than anyone else. He was a democrat at heart." It was this belief in the equality of humans that enabled him to believe that he could actually visit Stalin in Moscow and convince him of the need to change Soviet strategy in Southeast Asia. His personality was such that he attempted in all seriousness what others would have dismissed out of hand.

Judith was thirteen when her mother died, and her father became an overwhelming presence in her life. He encouraged her in debating at school, and convinced her of the intellectual and moral joys of studying Law at university. She grew up listening to him talk about politics at home and while visiting his friends, such as the Marshalls. Overwhelmed by the strength of his opinions and his choice of words in phrasing them, "I slavishly accepted everything that he said for a long time. I still think the way in which he thought although I am more cynical than he was. He had a strong belief in the innate goodness of human beings but I see more ulterior motives. He was very liberal; I have become rather more conservative over the years", she adds. "But I agree with him on the status of human beings, on how you should value people by what they are and not by their background, race or nationality."

Judith, who is married to lawyer Jaya Prakash and has four daughters, says that the fact she never wanted to emigrate was a result of her father's love for Singapore. De Cruz, who spent a year in the United States on a fellowship, was shocked by the violence and the racism that he witnessed there. "With his usual hyperbole, he used to tell Americans critical of Singapore that he lived in Paradise and they lived in Hell."

Judith grows wistful as the interview draws to a close. Given de Cruz's analytical ability and eloquence, "he could have been as good a lawyer as David Marshall" if he had had "a little more discipline" and studied further. "But if he gone on to be a lawyer, I doubt that I would have been born. He would have gone before the War, he would have been stuck in England during the War like my uncle was, he would have come back here and probably never met my mother because he met my mother when he was rabble-rousing in Malaya, and we really don't know what would have happened."

"Life did not treat him fairly", she says, but adds: "Life does not treat anybody fairly." It was partly de Cruz and partly his circumstances that prevented him from rising higher. Yet, he lived on his own terms. "He was an idealistic dreamer; that is what he was. He had no money sense and was never secure financially, but he was all right. He believed that what he needed would come, and somehow it did." Anyway, his was not a wishy-washy, placid life. Instead, it was marked by warmth, joy, and his ability to find anybody and everybody interesting. "Sometimes I wondered how he could put up with the tedium of some people. But old ladies loved him; young children loved him."

Simon Tensing de Cruz was twelve when his mother died. Judith, he says, was "the smart one, guaranteed to succeed and steady, followed all the rules, and never caused any trouble." By contrast, de Cruz did not believe that Simon, his second child, was doing his best, and did not spare the rod, but made it a point to say that any punishment he meted out hurt him more than it hurt Simon. "I could not hold a grudge against him for long. He had more faith in me than I had in myself. That is why he was disappointed when I did not take school seriously." Simon got into Raffles Institution because of his father, who convinced principal Philip Liau to give him a chance. Gerald de Cruz helped Simon with his study of literature, typing treatises on English poets such as Chaucer, Donne, Wordsworth, Shelley and Byron, which Simon adapted faithfully for his answers. That led to an "A" for one of his pre-university papers when he had been expected to fail. His father also gave him an "insider's view" on politics, which helped him score well in political science, his main subject at university. But "he failed to teach me mathematics". "It is not that he did not try to teach me at all: He did try his best to do so on several occasions, spending a couple of hours each time, trying to explain how certain solutions were arrived at. It was just that I couldn't grasp figures — a mental block. He lost his famous short temper a couple of times because of this! Mathematics was not his strong point either, unlike literature, but he made a great effort to try to tutor me."

"My father was a good example of how one should live: with no limits and no regrets. He represents trying to do the best you can, whatever you do", the retired Singapore diplomat says. "He was also a master at helping others. I am trying to do this myself now as a volunteer after having taken early retirement from the Ministry of Foreign Affairs. It has always been a bit of a disappointment to me that I am not more like my father — his gregariousness, his deep intellect, his amazing sense of humour. He was also so good with children: He attracted them like a magnet. I don't seem to have this facility. But as my father would say: 'Just be yourself and try to do your best.'" However, his father was second to none in coming to his defence when he thought that his son had been wronged. Simon was "an undisciplined young man" in his early secondary years at St. Patrick's School, he recalls. His long hair was a sign of his teenage defiance of authority. He ignored several warnings from his teachers to keep his hair short, and one day, two of them cut it forcibly. "My father was very upset, believing that the act infringed my human rights and could cause me emotional trauma later in life." A lawyer's letter, penned most probably by David Marshall, was despatched promptly to the school. The teachers panicked and apologized to Simon. By contrast, the father of a school friend whose hair, too, had been cut thought that the teachers had done the right thing. Although, like the other father, Gerald de Cruz did not want his son to be a rebellious youngster, he was implacable in defending his rights when he believed that authority had overstepped its legitimate bounds.

Simon de Cruz remembers his father writing to him from the United States and proclaiming his respect for the achievements of that country except for its race relations and penchant for violence. "He empathized with the situation of blacks", Simon says, and recalls the day in Singapore when his father brought home — which was at that time in Haig Road — a black American athlete whom he had befriended. Their visitor was overcome with emotion at this unexpected hospitality in a foreign country. Gerald de Cruz did the same for a young white European couple whom he had found painting a sidewalk to raise money — an activity that could have got them into trouble with the law. "He brought them home and gave them dinner, mainly, I think, to get them off the sidewalk."

Gerald de Cruz influenced his son's thoughts about Catholicism, communism and nation-building. "My father and mother — who, too, had left the Church — were partially the reason why I am not a Catholic. I am very anti-communist because communism captivated my father and then betrayed him. I believe that democracy is a better ideology than communism; indeed, democracy is the least worst of all ideologies", Simon declares. His father's conversion to Islam did not have much of an impact on him because by then "I had formed my own opinions. I was not upset when he became a Muslim because I knew that he was in love with my stepmother and it [the conversion] was something that he had to do." However, Simon adds, his father did not become a Muslim just to get married. "He delved into the religion, studied it, and tried to live by it. I stayed the way I was; finding my own way with my own mind." Gerald de Cruz's strongest influence on his son lay in strengthening his identity. "My father saw himself as a member of the human race. In fact, he wrote "Human" under the category "Race" on official forms. He did not see himself primarily as a Eurasian, did not consider himself a Eurasian leader, made fun of white Eurasians who considered themselves superior to others, and did not raise my sister and me as Eurasians. I grew up seeing myself as a Singaporean", Simon says.

Summing up Gerald de Cruz's legacy to Singapore, Simon says that it was his "fervent belief in the need to build up Singapore as a nation and a democracy. He was ahead of his times in thinking politically about Singapore's future, and this was not something that everyone in the Establishment was willing to hear." His father's abiding value to Singapore lies in his sense of mission, which took him from communism to Islam and democracy. "He did not harbour high ambitions and he certainly was not an opportunist. He searched for the truth for himself, passionately and without half-measures." Did life treat him unfairly? "Some people treated my father unfairly," Simon replies, refusing to name names, "but life did not. He did not feel shackled by life but had a keen sense of *carpe diem* — seize the day. He enjoyed life because he lived it without regrets."

Gerald de Cruz's son-in-law, Jaya Prakash, too, believes that "he did not achieve his life's aims. Everything that he did arrived at a point and then did not move further." In that sense, "life probably treated him badly". "The worst thing that could have happened to him personally is not to have been alive to see the success of his children. It was fate's cruel way of subverting the completeness in happiness", Jaya Prakash says. Yet, de Cruz made the best of that incompleteness. He met it with the quiet resignation of a Stoic. Jaya Prakash remembers his father-in-law's suffering after his strokes when, semi-paralysed, the once fiercely independent man had to depend on his family to be bathed, fed and even scratched for an itch on his arms that he was incapable of getting to. Yet, de Cruz never complained about his illness; instead, every act of care was met with an unfailing "thank you". His deep sense of courtesy towards others, stemming from gratitude for their presence in his life, never deserted him even in his darkest days. He took life's blows with a grace that blunted their destructive edge.

This capacity for patience, encouraged by the care and concern shown by lasting friends such as President C.V. Devan Nair, was in keeping with the workings of the intellectual and moral universe that de Cruz inhabited. "He was a poet at heart, whose romanticism was reflected in his actions. He was about fair play at its extreme. He was against any type of fundamentalism. He had no malice, no religious or racial bigotry, and no interest in rituals. He was not overly religious but he was enormously spiritual. I found him to be a closet Hindu", Jaya Prakash, himself a Hindu, says. Far from objecting to his daughter being courted by a man of a different faith, de Cruz gave his blessings to their romance. He turned up for their wedding dressed exactly the way Jaya Prakash's father was dressed. De Cruz embodied the freedom from sectarian thinking and behaviour that he preached.

To this day, Jaya Prakash remembers his father-in-law's towering personality. "He was a formidable individual with a powerful intellect. He was one of the best public speakers whom

I have heard, who used his commanding voice and gestures to persuade his audience", he recalls of the occasions when, as a student, he heard de Cruz address school assemblies. Unlike his speeches, his writing was controlled and restrained, but both were driven by the companionship of intellect and feeling. The problem was that de Cruz "could not administer ideas, turn them into reality. He was a genius and an intellectual, but he did not possess discipline. His ideas moved constantly, and he did not distil and concretise them. He was not a groupie and was governed mainly by his ideas, but he could not find a framework for his contributions. He could have done much better had he had a think-tank to run."

To Maimunah, speaking on the phone from her home in Malacca, Gerald de Cruz was simply "the best man" whom she had ever met. "He was extremely generous to other people in word and deed", she adds, recalling how, during their time together in Sarawak, he would help rehabilitate young people on drugs who had run away from home. Apart from his work at the Sarawak Foundation and his *dakwah* — missionary — work trying to convert Dayaks to Islam, he loved attending *ceramahs*, or political sermons and rallies. The peace and tranquillity of Sarawak helped the family to bond.

Maimunah looked after de Cruz with unbroken devotion after his two strokes. Modestly, she argues that caring for him was easy because he would never lose his temper. "His religious faith made him accept his strokes." But he appreciated her care "even on his deathbed", she says before breaking into sobs.

Adam de Cruz was born to Gerald and Maimunah in 1971. What the designer, who lives in London, knows about his father's political thinking is derived from reading *Rojak Rebel*. "My dad had suffered two strokes in my early teens. He had recovered completely from his first stroke but the second had left him slightly paralysed. It was during this time that he wrote his memoirs and that I learnt about his past", Adam recalls in an email interview. He remembers his father's "thirst for knowledge, his kindness and his spirit". "Forever optimistic, he was a really positive person to have around. There was always laughter and a huge smile. He was a very loving dad."

The Man of La Mancha was a family man after all.

Note

1. This chapter is based on interviews conducted with Gerald de Cruz's family members.

APPENDIX

Gerald de Cruz was a prolific writer. These two articles provide a taste of the subjects that interested him, and his style of writing.

New Nation, 21 September 1971

THEIR LEADERS MAY CHANGE, BUT SINO-SOVIET DISPUTE LOOKS SET TO GO ON FOREVER

"A Communist is a Communist is a Communist." said the bright and brash young man. "All the Russians and the Chinese have really been involved in, is a couple of skirmishes over their common border — and what's so inflammable about that? Isn't it normal on the part of neighbours to squabble?

"All the rest of it is merely verbal fireworks, a diversionary tactic to fool us into believing that they're enemies. At the right time they'll appear in their true light as fanatical Communist partners intent on world domination."

This question of the true relationship between the Soviet Union and the People's Republic of China is one of the most vital questions of the day.

It has become even more important in view of the modifications in Chinese foreign policy, the gradual emergence of detente between the United States and China, and the steady withdrawal of American forces from the Asian mainland.

If the bright young man is correct, then China will be able to bring tremendous concentration to bear soon on East and South-East Asia; if he is wrong, if the Soviet Union and China are really deeply involved in a contradiction of fundamental dimensions, then it is on its northern and north-western borders that the Chinese will have to focus their main attention.

I think he is completely wrong: I think that irrespective of what type of regime exists in either area, the contradictions between the two countries are of a fundamentally serious nature, with the deepest roots imaginable in geography, history, and contemporary imperatives. Mao has come and Mao will go, but the Sino–Soviet dispute bids fair to go on forever.

What is the Great Wall of China but man's longest (1500 miles) monument to fear and insecurity? Begun in 300 B.C. which is 2,300 years ago, it was first linked into a continuous line in the second century B.C. by the great unifier, Shih Huang Ti, first emperor of the Chin Dynasty.

What is the Great Wall of China but the strongest evidence possible that for the last 2000 years China has feared invasion from the north-west?

And what is the high plateau of Mongolia but a double-edged sword ready to be plunged deep into either Russia or China or both — as with Genghis Khan?

Neither the Soviet Union, over whose peoples the Mongols ruled implacably for two centuries, nor the Chinese will ever forget that they are both vulnerable to invasion from the Mongolian heartland of Asia, the "hinge of the world."

While the Chinese reaction was defensive (the Great Wall), the Russian reaction was to push their eastern boundaries as far to the east as possible, until they reached Vladivostock and the Sea of Japan.

This has involved them in innumerable wars with the Chinese.

In the 19th century, when Britain and France and Japan began their imperialistic capers in China, Russia took advantage of Chinese preoccupation with the western "barbarians" to build the Trans-Siberian railroad, its major instrument of penetration into Manchuria; to reduce Korea into a "protectorate"; and to take over Manchuria.

The Russians even took advantage of Sun Yat Sen's revolution in 1912 to consolidate their position in northern Manchuria, develop a large, new and important city in Harbin and support the Mongolians in their revolt against China.

Two thousand years of history, in which China has constantly been subjected to attack and invasion from the north and northwest, are not easy to forget.

Even in modern times, when China developed its own Communist Party, the revolutionary situation was so unlike that in Russia before the Bolshevik coup, that Russian advice to fight Chiang Kai-shek from the towns proved almost fatal for the Chinese Communists.

The Maoist revolution, built on a rural base, was a rescue operation that barely managed to haul Communism to the comparative safety of Yenan, several thousands of miles away from the eastern seaboard, from where it painfully began its comeback.

The conflict between the Soviet Union and China has roots, then, that go deeper than 2000 years in history, poisoning the relationship between these two Communist giants.

To add to their historical enmity, there is this 5000-mile border — this geographical reality of the long festering sore of a border which the Soviet side claims is unalterable, and which the Chinese side claims is "unequal and unjust."

These are not two neighbours bickering over a fence. When a fence is 5000 miles long, the people on either side of it stop being neighbours and start being enemies, especially when one party claims that the other has set up his fence deep in the territory of the first party.

Is it any wonder that there have been at least 5000 major and minor clashes between Soviet and Chinese troops along this border since 1960? Or that, according to reports, the Soviets have deployed one million men supported by the most modern weapons, including nuclear ones, in defence of it? Or that Chinese deployment is at least as great but probably much greater?

The situation has been further aggravated by the coming of Chinese Communism into power in 1949. National interests in such a situation must take precedence over and even dictate ideological strategy.

If a little Hungary or a tiny Czechoslovakia find national interests intolerably opposed to Soviet hegemony, how much more true must this be of Communist China.

There can be no kowtowing to the Soviet Union of any kind, and this includes ideology because it has a special Importance to Communists.

Their ideology is their legitimacy — it provides the rationale and the justification for their revolutionary seizure of power. Without it they would be revealed as pure and simple tyrants, without an ethic, purpose or plan.

To subordinate oneself to the Soviet Union ideologically would be to surrender the legitimacy of the regime into Soviet custody, and to reduce China into a lackey of the Soviet Union. Merely to state this, is to realise its absurdity.

The ideological controversy is, consequently no pyrotechnic camouflage behind which the Red giants are co-operating to bring the world to their feet.

It is a grim struggle behind which the Chinese revolution is trying to maintain its legitimacy and its sovereignty which, in this sense, are threatened not by the West but by the Soviet

Union. It only needs to be mentioned that the Soviet Union finds itself under the same threat from China to get an inkling of how serious the ideological exchange is.

The controversy between the two countries is made up of historical, geographical, ideological and national elements which, reinforcing one another, confront the world with the spectacle of an insoluble contradiction that will bedevil the relations between the two states for a long time.

We may come, I think, to the following conclusions:

First, that whether or not there is a change of regime in either state, the fundamental areas or conflict between them will not disappear;

Second, that "moderate" foreign policies by either or both states will temper but cannot solve these contradictions;

Third, that all Chinese experience has taught the Chinese to beware the winds from the northwest, and their suspicions must be intensified now that, on the other side of that border, they have to contend, not with nomads, but with another Communist giant as tough, dedicated and fanatical as themselves;

Fourth, that the Chinese determination today to re-enter the international community will tend to develop new areas of contradiction and conflict between them, as the announcement of President Nixon's proposed visit to China is proving;

Fifth, that more dissension and polycentrism will grow inside world Communism;

And finally, that the net result of all this will be more room for manoeuvre in the battle of survival by small states like ours.

New Nation, 12 September 1972

THE UGLY AND AMORAL BOMB CULTURE SPAWNED AT HIROSHIMA AND NAGASAKI

First the nightmarish horror and shock of the act itself perpetrated against the colourful backdrop of the Olympics: the sense of tragic futility, of wanton taking of life, of the cutting down in their prime of Israel's most athletic sons; of the staunchless flowing of rich, vigorous blood; of the waste, the terrible waste; then the fear, the knotting fear that clawed and twisted inside the stomach.

Why the fear? Because the killings are yet another urgent reminder that, side by side with the ordinary, beautiful culture of our times stalks an extraordinary, ugly culture, that, side by side with the morality of the ten commandments or their equivalent learned at mother's knee, stalks a deeper amorality whose obscene shadow now envelops a world grown small and apparently powerless to prevent the heartless crimes of the soulless killer.

And because, deep inside us, we have to admit that the two — the beautiful and and [*sic*] the perverse; the moral and the amoral — are bound together by the umbilical cord whose name is Science or Progress or Modernity.

The criminal insanity of the Nazis, their vicious "super-race" philosophy, and their use of gas chambers to eliminate millions, horrified the world: they were outlaws and they were punished as such.

But when a champion of democracy, one which had sacrificed so much to uphold the sacredness of the Individual against the Nazi madmen, and whose own philosophy celebrated the intrinsic, priceless worth of the Individual and his inalienable rights to life, liberty and the pursuit of happiness — when that power dropped the atom bombs to obliterate two Japanese towns, Hiroshima and Nagasaki, and in the process also obliterated friend and foe alike, young and old, the about-to-be-born, the poor, the sick, the crippled, all the Innocents — ON PURPOSE then the question arises: what and where is sanity?

Suddenly we lived in a different, shocking and terribly dangerous world, a world where the end we sought justified any and every means to that end; a world in which fascists, communists and democrats alike, when the needs arose, put the same amoral philosophy into practice, again and again and again.

For what is the building and the stockpiling of nuclear weapons by both totalitarian and democratic powers but crushing testimony to the supremacy of the Bomb Culture to which all the super-powers bend the knee?

I believe in God, the common man and the Bomb, profess the Americans: I believe In Matter, the proletariat and the Bomb, profess the Russians and the Chinese.

Is it any wonder, then, that beneath this amoral umbrella gradually grew up small groups of ruthless men, whom we now call urban guerillas, who practise unlimited terror to achieve their ends? To call them savages is to slander the "savages" and to miss the real point — that these are modern men, using the most modern weapons, limited by no ethical, moral or religious code — the spawn of the Bomb Culture.

(Sanctified by the deliberate dropping of the atom bombs on Hiroshima and Nagasaki, this ugly, amoral culture has been appropriately named the Bomb Culture.)

Before the Bomb Culture there were still limits to the means we used to achieve our ends, and if we exceeded them we paid the penalty most of the time. Today these limits have disappeared.

If the obliteration of innocent lives by the Bomb is permissible, then everything is permissible. This is what underlies the "permissive society," our condemnation of which will never modify or change it if at the same time we swallow the Bomb and its culture — that the use of unlimited terror against men, women and children is permitted to achieve our ends.

It is true that men have always lived by killing. We kill to eat, we kill for pleasure, we kill for sport, we kill for gain, we kill for kicks, we kill above all in war — but always before there were limits and penalties — set by law, custom or precedent.

Today, under the Bomb Culture, there are no limits anywhere, anymore. All is permitted: this is what the Bomb means. There are still laws, of course, against killing, but the very countries which make those laws also make the Bombs, or are linked with the powers that make and stockpile the Bombs, demonstrating the existence of the parallel cultures, the moral, and the amoral.

I use the capital B for Bomb to remove any misunderstanding. I am referring to nuclear weapons which can wipe out entire cities, entire nations, all civilised life, in a few hours.

Non-nuclear bombs cannot do this, as well but tragically exemplified in North Vietnam where the sustained air bombardment of the Americans — the most powerful and devastating of its kind — has not succeeded in destroying the will of the North Vietnamese to fight on, let alone obliterate them as a people.

Total obliteration is what the use of nuclear weapons can accomplish, and while such bombs exist they negate the laws, the decencies, the moralities, the limits we impose on our lives in order to survive with some dignity. While they continue to exist we may say that terror is "sanctified"; the amoral soullessness of urban guerillas everywhere is "sanctified": the terrorism of the Arab guerillas is "sanctified."

How desperately difficult, almost impossible it is for us to accept that the amoral Arab guerillas, striking down innocent people at will anywhere and everywhere, or the equally amoral desperadoes of Latin America — are not outside the Establishment but well within it; that they are expert manipulators of the end-justifies-the-means philosophy which lies behind the use and stockpiling of nuclear bombs. But acceptance of this fact is the pre-requisite to the destruction of the Bomb Culture and its vile practitioners.

(The postman arrives and brings me the latest issue of New Q, the journal of the Student Christian Movement in Singapore. On its front page is a poem in which God speaks: "I jump on mines, I gasp my last breath in foxholes; I moan, riddled with shrapnel... I sweat men's blood on battlefields ... while around me men keep on shouting, singing, dancing, and as if insane crucify me in an enormous burst of laughter... It matters not whether you are among those who hit or among those who watch ... you are all guilty...").

Does that partly explain the indescribable clutch of fear in my stomach as I watched the news of the slaughter of the Israeli athletes in Munich? That I know, deep in my bowels, that the world has gone insane? Perhaps the Soviet Union is correct to lock up its critics and dissenters in mental hospitals, for where else should the sane take refuge in a schizophrenic world?

And the guilt. We are guilty for not doing enough to compel the banning and the destruction of the Bomb, thus smashing the foundations of the Bomb Culture. That is the inevitable first step. We will have to renew, all over the world, the spirit of the Ban-the-Bomb Aldermaston marchers, a spirit which was much more than an old-fashioned peace march, or a protest one.

"It was," Christopher Driver wrote, "a civilising mission, a march away from fear towards normality, towards human standards, towards the real people in the nursery rhyme whose houses are over the hill and not so far away that we cannot get there by candlelight, whose hands are set to the plough and the making of things."

I remember a story told of Mahatma Gandhi which has an important lesson for us. When he walked through the Indian country-side he often swerved, taking a zig-zag course although there were no discernible obstacles in his path. One day a disciple asked him why he walked in that manner.

"I was avoiding the ants," replied Gandhi. "They, too, have a right to life."

INDEX

Note: Pages numbers followed by "n" refer to notes.

ABOUT THE AUTHOR

Asad-ul Iqbal Latif is the author of several books, including *Lim Kim San: A Builder of Singapore* (2009) and *Wang Gungwu: Junzi: Scholar-Gentleman in Conversation with Asad-ul Iqbal Latif* (2010), and a co-editor of *George Yeo on Bonsai, Banyan and the Tao* (2015). He graduated with Honours in English from Presidency College, Calcutta, and received his Master of Letters degree in History at Clare Hall, Cambridge, where he was Raffles (Chevening) and S. Rajaratnam Scholar. He was a Fulbright Visiting Scholar at Harvard University's Weatherhead Center for International Affairs. A former journalist, he worked at *The Statesman* in Calcutta, *Asiaweek* in Hong Kong, and *The Business Times* and *The Straits Times* in Singapore. He was a Jefferson Fellow at the East-West Center in Hawaii.

Gerald de Cruz's parents, circa 1919.

With his wife, Coral, in Europe, 1949.

With Coral and Stanley Stewart, later Head of the Civil Service, 1951.

With Coral and friends, early 1960s.

Political Study Centre, with G.G. Thomson on his left, 1960s.

With G.G. Thomson on a visit to Sarawak, 1960s.

Visit of Puan Noor Aishah, wife of President Yusof bin Ishak, to a centre run by the Singapore Association for Mentally Retarded Children, 1960s.

With Coral (right), daughter Judith and son Simon, Hastings, 1954.

Attending a trade union conference in Nigeria, November 1965.

With son Simon and de Cruz's cousin, Linda Kraal, at the Istana, early 1965.

Gesticulating during a talk, 1970s.

At wedding reception with David Marshall (left), bride Maimunah and Mrs Jean Marshall (right), December 1970.

With President C.V. Devan Nair, Kuching.

With President Yusof bin Ishak at the Istana, early 1965.

At a school function, 1970s.

With NTUC founder C.V. Devan Nair and Prime Minister Lee Kuan Yew at the modernisation seminar.

Addressing the seminar.

At a trade union gathering.

With David Marshall, mid-1970s.

With David Marshall's brother, Meyer, mid-1970s.

With Maimunah and son Adam, Singapore, 1972.

With children Judith and Simon, Singapore, 1972.

Gerald de Cruz's deep humanism, his love of life, and his astringent literary style come through in this selection from his poems.

LITTLE TIME LEFT

Tell our stories

now

there's little time left

to see

or hear

or to be cleft

with pain

and love

tell our stories

now

~~STRIKE~~

The Knife of truth

Strike
knife of truth
deep into my heart
cut it out
it's only something
that ticks
its ticking now
a psychological reflex
and little more

this that I call
me
is only the appearance
of one who stands
and breathes
alive as a shadow
is alive
dead as a shadow is dead

Strike
knife true and deep
cut out too
the agile tongue of me
which works
overtime
to build a screen of words
around my walking death

my tongue's a leaf
that rustles and quivers
on a withered tree
blown about by wayward
winds dipping and bowing
to every fretful gust
a labial rattle
from a shadow
dressed to look like
a man

Strike
into this sapless tree
cut deep knife
to find
if there be one cell
out of billions trillions
untainted undefiled
sapful
from which life
and man
may yet be born

———

THE PROMISED LAND

What is the use of your passports
when my skin is black
this is the real passport
to my daily rack

What is the use of your promises
when my skin is black
every promise broken
blood seeps through the crack

What is the use of your money
when my skin is black
money cannot ~~buy~~ save the Dream
~~or bring my voices back~~ ~~children~~
from dying on my back

THE TRUTH

A lie is, after all,
a kind of truth,
and sometimes kinder
when truth is not kind.

Justice is, after all,
a kind of love,
and sometimes kinder
when love is not kind.

Death is, after all,
a kind of life,
and sometimes kinder
when life is not kind.

ALTHOUGH I OBTAINED GRADE ONE IN THE SENIOR CAMBRIDGE EXAM

~~There are~~ of the two hundred and twenty-two

wayside trees

between Siglap Road and town

I only know

the names

of two

on the way up

and none

on the way

down.

www.ingramcontent.com/pod-product-compliance
Lightning Source LLC
Chambersburg PA
CBHW071854270326
41929CB00013B/2225

* 9 7 8 9 8 1 4 6 2 0 6 8 0 *